As Local Studies Librarian at the Cheshire Record Office, no one could be better qualified than Peter Bamford to be the author of a book on the county's curiosities. Although Lancashire born and bred, he has worked in Chester for the past eighteen years and lived there for most of that time. He enjoys making a hobby out of his work (and vice versa), walking in the countryside, and modelling ships in bottles. His wife and two children all regard one or more of these activities as somewhat eccentric.

Frontispiece
Elephant & Castle, Peckforton (see No 55).

Cheshire Curiosities

Peter Bamford

THE DOVECOTE PRESS

To June, the driving force behind this book.

First published in 1992 by The Dovecote Press Ltd
Stanbridge, Wimborne, Dorset BH21 4JD

ISBN 0 946159 96 3

© Peter Bamford 1992

Phototypeset in Times by The Typesetting Bureau Ltd
Wimborne, Dorset
Printed and bound in Singapore

Contents

Introduction

What constitutes a curiosity is essentially a matter of subjective judgment, and so I do not expect anyone who knows Cheshire to agree, necessarily, with my own choice. More objectively, however, it can be said that the 80 "curiosities" contained in this book can all be viewed (from the outside at least) at any reasonable time of day and without payment of an admission charge.

The scope is that of the post-1974 county, with an emphasis on rural sites. Chester itself has been entirely excluded, not because it lacks curiosities, but because it is already well served by guides.

I should like to express my gratitude to my wife June, who, in the course of the book's compilation, drove me round Cheshire while I drove her round the bend. Likewise to Isobel and Eric Duncan, companions on a number of photographic forays. My thanks are also due to Carole Carden and Maureen Cook for painlessly extracting the typescript from my hand-writing, and to Steve Howe of The Black and White Picture Place, Chester, for applying his darkroom skills to my negatives. For permission to reproduce non-photographic illustrations, and colour transparencies, I am grateful to Cheshire Libraries, Arts and Archives and to Cheshire Tourism and Marketing, respectively. Last but not least, thank you to all my present and past colleagues at the Cheshire Record Office and Chester Library for their help and support over many years.

A final word: some of the curiosities described are private residences, so please respect the occupiers' privacy. Others are situated on or near narrow roads; please park your car safely and considerately. The public footpaths which lead to some others do not normally require the wearing of boots, though obviously the ground may be muddy in wet weather. A study of the relevant Ordnance Survey Map may well indicate a circular walk which can incorporate a visit to a curiosity. Please do try this, as it can often be the best approach, and you might come across something which strikes you as even more curious!

Peter Bamford

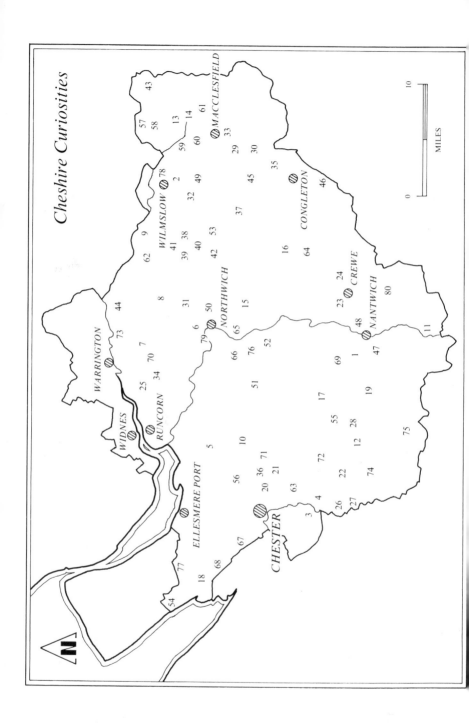

Cheshire Curiosities

N

MILES

0   10

WARRINGTON

WIDNES

RUNCORN

ELLESMERE PORT

CHESTER

WILMSLOW

MACCLESFIELD

NORTHWICH

CONGLETON

CREWE

NANTWICH

43
57
58
13
14
61
59
60
33
29
30
35
78
2
49
32
45
46
9
38
37
16
64
41
53
62
39 40 42
44
8
31
50
15
23 24
6
65
48
80
73
79
66 76 52
11
7
70
51
69 1 47
25
34
17
19
55
28
5
10
12
75
56 36 71
72
20 21
22
74
63
4 26 27
3
18
67
77
68
54

1 The End of the Game?

Position: Acton, near Nantwich
Ordnance Map: Stoke-on-Trent and Macclesfield area: Sheet 118: 1/50,000
Map Ref: SJ 631/530
Access: At the side of Acton churchyard nearest to the A.5017 road.

Noticeable from the road is an old tomb surrounded by railings, and a few yards to the north of this stands a white marble cross which marks the grave of Albert Neilson Hornby (1847-1925).

Hornby was the archetypal Victorian gentleman cricketer. Of a Lancashire family, though living at Nantwich, he played (as an amateur) for Nantwich, Lancashire (which he captained) and England (likewise). In fact it was Hornby who was the England captain during the 1882 Test Match against Australia which gave birth to the Ashes.

Albert Hornby's grave, Acton churchyard.

It is not the cross, conspicuous though it is, which is the curious feature of the grave. Hornby himself was apparently responsible for the design of the horizontal white marble tombstone. This features, carved in relief, a cricket bat, ball, stumps and bails, plus Hornby's signature. Not only is it a clear statement of his consuming passion in this life, but the fact that the wicket is intact suggests that A.N. Hornby did not regard death as the end of his innings.

Places of Interest in the Neighbourhood
47. A Sacrifice Still Remembered (Nantwich)
48. From the Ashes of a Vehement Fire (Nantwich)
69. Stoke Hall Dovecote (Stoke)

2 The Wizard and Mr. Garner

Position: Alderley Edge, near Wilmslow
Ordnance Map: Stoke-on-Trent and Macclesfield area: Sheet 118:
1/50,000
Map Ref: SJ 854/781
Access: On north side of the Edge, overlooking Mottram Road. Walk
up Squirrel's Jump, follow path gradually rising until it dips down to a
track junction. The path then rises more steeply up steps to the right.
When the gradient eases, and the path bears left, you encounter the
Wizard's Well on your right.

The story of the Wizard of Alderley Edge and the Iron Gates is a local
variant of the widespread folktale of the band of sleeping warriors in a
subterranean chamber, awaiting the call which will bring them forth
to save their country in a time of crisis. The Alderley version can be
traced back probably to the mid-17th century, although the first printed
version did not appear until 1805.

It probably acquired a wider circulation when Manchester cotton
magnates began building their houses here in the 1840s. This was the
period when the London and North Western Railway was offering a
free pass, valid for 21 years, between Alderley and Manchester, to
anyone who built a residence with a rateable value of £50 or more
within one mile of Alderley station.

The Edge is nowadays studded with sites allegedly connected with the
legend, or of a more general folklore significance. They are generally
assumed to have been there since the remote past, until, that is,
children's author Alan Garner, a native of the area, claimed (in the
March 1991 issue of *Cheshire Life*) that a couple, at least, were the work
of his great-great-grandfather Robert Garner, a local stonemason.

He, it was, apparently, who carved the face of the wizard in the rock,
and the inscription:

DRINK OF THIS
AND TAKE THY FILL
FOR THE WATER FALLS
BY THE WIZHARD'S WILL

The Druid's Circle, about half a mile along the path to the south-east,
was likewise erected by him: his reason was simply that he wanted to get
rid of some old stones!

What Mr. Garner's motives were can only be guessed at. Presumably

11

he did well out of the mid-19th century building boom, but whether he was aiming to please'the rich incomers (sometimes referred to by the local gentry as "Cottontots") or cocking a snook at their gullibility, is not clear. Whatever the case, it is good to see both the legend and his tongue-in-cheek additions to it still surviving.

Places of Interest in the Neighbourhood
32. Contrasting Faces of a Baptist Chapel (Great Warford)
49. An Elizabethan Corn Mill (Nether Alderley)
78. Romany's Garden of Remembrance (Wilmslow)

Iron Bridge, Aldford.

3 An Original "Telford"

Position: Aldford, between Chester and Farndon
Ordnance Map: Chester, Wrexham and surrounding area: Sheet 117:
1/50,000
Map Ref: SJ 418/601
Access: By public footpath leading northwards from Aldford church: a
good view of the Iron Bridge can be obtained from the footpath on the
east bank of the River Dee.

This graceful cast-iron bridge was built in 1824 for Robert Grosvenor,
first Marquess of Westminster, of Eaton Hall. Its single span measures
151 feet. The builder was William Hazledine, whose name appears in
raised lettering on the carriageway band at the north side of the east end
of the bridge. The names of other people involved in its construction
can also be seen in similar positions at the other corners.

Hazledine carried out a great deal of ironwork for the noted engineer
Thomas Telford, and this bridge has many "Telford" features. In fact,
apart from the "Gothic work" in the spandrels, it is a copy of one which
Hazledine had built to Telford's design at Atcham, near Shrewsbury, in
1818.

Whether Telford was given official credit (or any payment) for the
design is not clear, but it seems fair to regard the bridge as being one of
his, if only indirectly. From that point of view, the Iron Bridge's
importance lies in the fact that all the other cast-iron bridges by Telford
have suffered from increasingly heavy traffic and have had to be
strengthened. Thus the Iron Bridge is the only example remaining
exactly as built, and since traffic across it is very light, it is likely to
remain so.

Places of Interest in the Neighbourhood
 4. The Duke's Dispensary (Aldford)
26. Recalling the Relief of Lucknow (Farndon)
27. The Roundheads' Gateway to Wales (Farndon)

4 The Duke's Dispensary

Position: Aldford, between Chester and Farndon
Ordnance Map: Chester, Wrexham and surrounding area: Sheet 117:
1/50,000
Map Ref: SJ 422/593
Access: Stocks View is on the B.5130 road, just north of the Grosvenor
Arms public house.

Aldford, like many villages beside this stretch of the River Dee, forms
part of the Eaton Estate of the Dukes of Westminster, whose seat is at
Eaton Hall across the river. Hugh Lupus Grosvenor, the first Duke,
was a considerable philanthropist, one of his major concerns being the
Jubilee Institute for Nurses, which he helped to found at the time of
Queen Victoria's Golden Jubilee in 1887. The Institute pioneered the
provision of district nurses for the care of the sick poor in their homes.
   Putting his principles into effect on his home ground, the Duke had
this pair of cottages built between 1893 and 1895. The left-hand one,
the present Stocks View (look for the stocks on the opposite side of
the road) was formerly Nurse's Cottage. A district nurse was accom-
modated there, and the single-storey section at the left of the cottage
was the dispensary.

Places of Interest in the Neighbourhood
  3. An Original "Telford" (Aldford)
 26. Recalling the Relief of Lucknow (Farndon)
 27. The Roundheads' Gateway to Wales (Farndon)

Stocks View (former nurse's cottage & dispensary), Aldford.

5 Moving House – Literally

Position: Alvanley, south-east of Helsby
Ordnance Map: Chester, Wrexham and surrounding area: Sheet 117: 1/50,000
Map Ref: SJ 509/735
Access: By public footpath from unclassified roads to north or south. Follow Sandstone Trail signs (a footprint bearing the letter S).

Nestled against the slope of Alvanley Cliff, Austerson Old Hall looks like an example of an old Cheshire timber-framed house (which it is), standing where it has stood for centuries (which it has not).

   The hamlet of Austerson is situated south of Nantwich, and it was there that the Hall was built, probably in the mid-sixteenth century, with the long wing being added a century or so later.

Austerson Old Hall, Alvanley.

In the early 1980s it was bought by a local architect, dismantled, and re-erected here. The reconstruction has been carried out with great care; where additional materials have been required, old bricks, tiles and so on have been used wherever possible.

Without wishing to understate the magnitude of the task, it is easier to move a timber-framed building such as this than a brick or stone structure. The frames would originally have been made by the carpenter, probably off-site, and marked in relation to each other, being given a trial assembly before being finally erected.

Places of Interest in the Neighbourhood
10. The Last Great Cockfight (Ashton)
56. From Hermit to Archbishop (Plemstall)

Anderton boat lift.

6 Unique in this Country – First in the World

Position: Anderton, north-west of Northwich
Ordnance Map: Stoke-on-Trent and Macclesfield area: Sheet 118:
1/50,000
Map Ref: SJ 647/753
Access: Small signs on the south side of the unclassified road through
Anderton village point to "ANDERTON BOAT LIFT". From the
parking space, cross the canal by footbridge: this brings you level with
the top of the lift. A path going downhill to the right takes you to the
bank of the Weaver, whence a more impressive view of the lift can be
obtained.

Anderton is the spot where the Trent and Mersey Canal and the Weaver
Navigation approach most closely to each other, and from the canal's
early days there has been transhipment of cargoes from the one to
the other. Direct access for boats was impossible, however, because
the level of the canal is 50 feet above that of the Weaver. Originally
the main commodity involved was salt from Middlewich, and this was
unloaded down chutes. But obviously it was in everyone's interest to
find a more economic and less labour-intensive method, and so in 1875
Leader Williams, who was engaged in modernising the Weaver Navigation, designed the Anderton lift.

There had been small boat lifts constructed on canals before the end
of the 18th century, but none had been really successful, and at best
they could only handle five-ton tub-boats. The Anderton lift, hydrauli-
cally operated, could take a full-size barge or a pair of narrowboats,
fully laden, and raise or lower them in five minutes, which not only
ensured its success, but made it the first major boat lift in the world.

It was converted to electrical operation between 1906 and 1908. A
century after its construction it was found to be suffering from corro-
sion problems, and had to be closed to traffic in 1983. Boat lifts like this
never really caught on in Britain, but the principle was enthusiastically
adopted on the continent, where the largest lift, at La Louviere in Bel-
gium, can take barges of 350 tons.

The Anderton lift is scheduled for restoration, and it is hoped that it
will soon be open to traffic once again, a triumph of Victorian civil
engineering which has been fittingly described as one of the wonders of
Cheshire.

Appleton Thorn.

7 Bawming the Thorn

Position: Appleton
Ordnance Map: Manchester and surrounding area: Sheet 109: 1/50,000
Map Ref: SJ 637/838
Access: At crossroads by Appleton Church.

The original Appleton thorn is said to have been planted in 1178 by
Adam de Dutton, a local knight and landowner. He had returned from
the Crusades by way of Glastonbury and had acquired an offshoot
from that abbey's famous thorn, which was said to have miraculously
sprouted from Joseph of Arimathaea's staff.

Sometime between then and the nineteenth century grew up the
custom, unique in England, of "Bawming the thorn", "bawming" being
a dialect word for "adorning". The ceremony basically consisted of
decorating the tree with fresh flowers and red ribbons, followed by
dancing round it in a circle.

The original tree, or a successor, stood here until some date prior to
1880. A.W. Boyd, who described the 1933 ceremony, was told that it
was moved to Arley Park. This may well have been the case, for in 1880
a new tree was planted by Mrs. Piers Egerton-Warburton on the occasion of her marriage. Her new father-in-law, who composed a song for
the occasion, was Rowland Egerton-Warburton, the "Rhyming Squire"
of Arley Hall.

The "bawming" custom seems to have died out some time after
Rowland's death in 1891. The festival was attracting an undesirable
element from Warrington and elsewhere. It was, however, revived as we
have seen, though it seems later to have lapsed once again.

The tree itself lasted until 1965, when it blew down. Its replacement
soon withered and died, and so the present tree, a cutting from the
Glastonbury thorn, was planted in October 1967, and is cared for by
the local Women's Institute.

The "bawming" ceremony was revived again in 1973. It is nowadays
carried out by children from the local primary school on or about June
29th, and the current "heritage" boom should ensure its continuation
for some time to come.

Places of Interest in the Neighbourhood
34. For Future Service or Recollection (Halton)
70. "Time Is Not All" (Stretton)
73. King Edward's Lost City (Thelwall)

8 Rhymes of a Fox Hunting Man

Position: Arley
Ordnance Map: Manchester and surrounding area: Sheet 109: 1/50,000
Map Ref: SJ 671/809
Access: On north side of unclassified road, just before the gate to Arley
Hall drive. There is a walkers' free car park signposted on the same side
of the road coming into Arley.

> Trespassers this notice heed
> Onward you may not proceed
> Unless to Arley Hall you speed

warns the wooden signboard by the gate. The lines were the
composition of Rowland Eyles Egerton-Warburton (1804-1891), the
"Rhyming Squire" of Arley. After Eton and Oxford, he made the
Grand Tour and then settled on his estate, to which he devoted great
care, rebuilding Arley Hall.

He was an extremely keen foxhunter, usually riding horses bred by
himself, and it was on the subject of hunting that his best-known poetry
was written. He began by writing songs and verses for the amusement
of his fellow-members of the Tarporley Hunt Club. These compositions
were collected and published in 1846 as "Hunting Songs", which went
through eight editions in his lifetime and have been occasionally
republished since. So active a man must have found the blindness from
which he suffered for the last seventeen years of his life (due to
glaucoma) a severe trial.

If you decide to pay the entrance fee to Arley Hall gardens, you will
see more of Rowland's rhyming signposts there. The boards are faithful
reproductions of the originals. His verses will also be encountered at
Great Budworth.

Places of Interest in the Neighbourhood
  7. Bawming the Thorn (Appleton)
31. Water with Some Body to It (Great Budworth)
44. "Careless, Intemperate and Improvident" (Lymm)

9 No Support for the Pretender

Position: Ashley Hall, Ashley, near Wilmslow
Ordnance Map: Manchester and surrounding area: Sheet 109: 1/50,000
Map Ref: SJ 769/849
Access: By public footpath from unclassified roads to north or south.

The gentry of Cheshire were long renowned for their loyalty to the reigning monarch, and many families suffered for their devotion during and after the Civil War. Accordingly, with the death of Queen Anne in 1714, the accession of George I, and then the Jacobite rising in favour of Prince James Edward Stuart in the autumn of 1715, they found themselves on the horns of a dilemma.

Ten leading Cheshire gentlemen, who were in the habit of meeting socially, got together to decide whether they were going to support King George as guardian of the established order and representative of constitutional government, or Prince James Edward as heir of the House of Stuart for which some of their ancestors had sacrificed much in the preceding century.

The meeting, attended by Sir Richard Grosvenor, James, Earl of Barrymore, Charles Hurleston, Amos Meredith, Alexander Radclyff, Robert Cholmondeley, John Warren, Henry Legh and Peter Legh, of Lyme, took place at Ashley Hall, then the residence of Thomas Assheton, the governor of Chester Castle. Peter Legh, who had been imprisoned in 1694 and again in 1696 on suspicion of treason against William of Orange, moved that no support be shown for the Stuart cause. After what must have been an intense debate, his motion was carried by the casting vote of Mr. Assheton.

After the defeat of the Jacobite forces at Preston and Sheriffmuir, the ten decided to celebrate their fortunate decision (which probably saved their estates, and possibly their lives) by having their portraits painted. The ten full-length pictures were painted in 1720 by an artist whose identity is not recorded. They remained in the large room at Ashley Hall until 1860, when Lord Egerton of Tatton, into whose family's possession the Hall had come, removed them to Tatton Hall, near Knutsford, where they now grace the staircase landing.

Places of Interest in the Neighbourhood
41. The Home of Higgins the Highwayman (Knutsford)
62. Paratroops Smelt Mermaid (Rostherne)
78. Romany's Garden of Remembrance (Wilmslow)

10 The Last Great Cockfight

Position: Ashton, north-west of Kelsall
Ordnance Map: Chester, Wrexham and surrounding area: Sheet 117:
1/50,000
Map Ref: SJ 498/697
Access: Peel Hall is accessible by public footpath from Gongar Lane,
the road to the east, or from the west side of Ashton village.

Cockfighting was officially declared illegal in 1849, but it certainly
continued on a considerable scale for some years thereafter. In the years
running up to 1865 many mains (as cockfights were called) had been
held in the Delamere Forest area, but so carefully had security been
observed that the police had never managed to be in the right place at
the right time.

The place on this occasion was the orchard at Peel Hall. The orchard
was conveniently surrounded by a nine feet high wall. At the orchard's
centre was a ring, about five yards in diameter, enclosed with turves,
and around this were benches, chairs, and logs of wood for spectators
to sit on.

The first two cocks were placed in the ring, under the supervision of
Joseph Beckett, the tenant of Peel Hall, and the fight began. It lasted
about fifteen minutes and was followed by an even more harrowing
twenty-minutes bout between two fresh cocks.

Before the third fight could begin, the Chief Constable and a force of
policemen pushed their way through the crowd and entered the ring.
Proceedings came to an abrupt halt, and the leading cockfighters, after
conferring together for some time, asked the police if they intended to
prosecute. On being assured that this was the intention, the cockfighters
decided that they might as well have their money's worth and said that
they would continue with their programme whatever the consequences.

Unbelievable as it seems today, the Chief Constable and his men then
stood aside while a further fifteen bouts were fought, before taking the
offenders into custody.

Twenty-four men appeared before the magistrates at Delamere on
25th April. Beckett was the only local man – the others came from as
far away as Bolton, Worcester and Islington. Fines were imposed of £5
and £2 10s. 0d., with the alternative of a month's imprisonment with
hard labour.

That was the incredible end of cockfighting in the Delamere Forest
area, but there is evidence that the horrible sport continued well into

this century in Cheshire, and it is said that it has not entirely died out
even yet.

Places of Interest in the Neighbourhood
  5. Moving House – Literally (Alvanley)
 36. Where Packhorses Plodded (Hockenhull Platts)
 56. From Hermit to Archbishop (Plemstall)
 71. The Incomparable Penman (Tarvin)

11 Butchers, Butter and Bears

Position: Audlem
Ordnance Map: Stoke-on-Trent and Macclesfield area: Sheet 118:
1/50,000
Map Ref: SJ 659/436
Access: In the Square, in front of the church.

Close to the churchyard steps stands a structure which could easily pass
for a bus shelter, an impression heightened by the benches which it
contains. It is in fact the town's Market Hall. Built about 1733, its style,
particularly the eight Tuscan pillars, looks rather earlier – an example
of how fashions changed slowly in the provinces.

What goods were sold there seems uncertain; the building is sometimes called the Shambles, but Audlem writers generally refer to it as
the Butter Market. More certain, however, is the origin of the large
stone block nearby. It is the Bear Stone, and incorporated an iron ring
to which a bear would be tethered before bear-baiting was outlawed. It
originally stood in the centre of the Square, on the spot now occupied
by the lamp standard and monument to Richard Baker Bellyse, a
doctor who served Victorian Audlem for forty years.

Places of Interest in the Neighbourhood
47. A Sacrifice Still Remembered (Nantwich)
48. From the Ashes of a Vehement Fire (Nantwich)
80. The Time and the Inclination (Wybunbury)

Market Hall, Audlem.

12 The Best of British Castramentation

Position: Bickerton, south-east of the A41/A534 intersection at Broxton
Ordnance Map: Chester, Wrexham and surrounding area: Sheet 117: 1/50,000
Map Ref: SJ 498/529
Access: By sign-posted footpath from the Sandstone Trail information board at Duckington (Map Ref: SJ 494/524).

Maiden Castle is the southernmost of a chain of prehistoric earth-works situated on or near Cheshire's central sandstone ridge. It possesses commanding views to the west, where the ridge falls away steeply, and on that side it needed no artificial defences. Its eastern flank is protected by a double rampart which is turned inwards at the entrance to deepen the defences at that vulnerable point. At the time it was occupied, the absence of trees would have made the view even more impressive.

A pre-Roman Iron Age structure, its earliest phase probably dates from the first century B.C. The outer rampart was reconstructed and strengthened, probably about 50-75 A.D., in response to the threat from the advancing legions of Rome.

Excavations between 1932 and 1935 produced one important find – a small piece of iron which established, for the first time, that the idea of the hillfort and knowledge of iron had reached Cheshire before the Romans.

George Ormerod, the historian of Cheshire, described Maiden Castle in 1819 as "one of the most perfect specimens of British castramentation in Cheshire". If you walk to the east of the path across Bickerton Hill, near the National Trust plaque, you can see and follow the line of the two ramparts, each of which would originally have been at least 20 feet wide by 10 feet high. As you walk, you can try to imagine the feelings of the Britons of nearly two thousand years ago as they gazed along the ancient way through the Bickerton Gap and watched for the approach of the Romans.

Places of Interest in the Neighbourhood
22. Hot Jewellery (Clutton)
28. The Copper Mine Chimney (Gallantry Bank)
55. The Elephant and Castle (Peckforton)

13 Symbol of Bollington's Industrial Past

Position: Bollington
Ordnance Map: Stoke-on-Trent & Macclesfield area: Sheet 118: 1/50,000
Map Ref: SJ 937/781
Access: On the south side of Green Lane, though conspicuous from almost anywhere in Bollington.

This octagonal tower-like structure, with a castellated balcony just below its top, looks like some sort of watchtower. Its real purpose was completely different – it is (or was) a factory chimney.

Bollington used to be a cotton town, and the chimney was built in the early nineteenth century to serve the former Oak Bank Mill, which stood at the bottom of the slope on the chimney's south side. A conventional chimney would have had to be impossibly tall, so this relatively short (and attractive) one was built and connected to the mill's boiler by a tunnel flue.

Places of Interest in the Neighbourhood
14. White Nancy (Bollington)
59. An Early Exercise in Conservation (Prestbury)
60. Once a Vicarage – Now a Bank (Prestbury)
61. The Mystery of the Woman's Footprint (Rainow)

14 White Nancy

Position: Bollington
Ordnance Map: Stoke-on-Trent and Macclesfield area: Sheet 118:
1/50,000
Map Ref: SJ 939/771
Access: From the Redway Tavern (Map Ref: SJ 937/771).

This well-known local landmark stands 920 feet above sea level at the
northern end of Kerridge Hill, astride the boundary between the civil
parishes (and ancient townships) of Bollington and Rainow. The facts
surrounding its construction are known, but are often obscured by
folklore and mystery.

It was built in 1817 to commemorate the Battle of Waterloo at the
behest of John Gaskell of North End Farm, to the east. He apparently
intended it for a folly, a summer-house, and possibly also a boundary
marker. About twenty feet high, it is hollow inside and originally had a
door into the interior, which contained a circular stone table in the
centre and stone benches around the edge. Unfortunately, twentieth
century vandalism has led to the doorway being blocked up and plas-
tered over.

Local fancy has led to other reasons being given for its construction:

White Nancy.

as a lovers' trysting-place (a bit conspicuous, surely?) or as a quiet place for meditation.

How White Nancy got her name is something of a mystery. Some accounts say she was named after a lady of the Gaskell family, others after the leading horse of the team of eight that dragged up the hill the huge circular stone slab that was used for the table inside. A third theory makes the 'Nancy' part of the name a pun on 'Ordnance', referring to the Ordnance Survey, whose triangulation column stands at the southern end of Kerridge Hill, but the structure is mentioned as 'Northern Nancy' in 1825, and the Ordnance Survey did not begin its work here until some fifteen years later.

White Nancy is conspicuous over a wide area – indeed pilots are said to use her for a 'fix' on Manchester Airport, but to see her at close quarters start from the Redway Tavern mentioned above. From the pub car park a footpath sign points up a concrete-surfaced track. Follow this across a cattle grid, then turn immediately right up a path which, though steep, is quite distinct. Soon you will see the white ball finial which crowns Nancy in view on the skyline. Once you have reached her, take in the view at your leisure before retracing your steps.

Places of Interest in the Neighbourhood
13. Symbol of Bollington's Industrial Past (Bollington)
59. An Early Exercise in Conservation (Prestbury)
60. Once a Vicarage – Now a Bank (Prestbury)
61. The Mystery of the Woman's Footprint (Rainow)

15 The Centre of Cheshire?

Position: Bostock Green
Ordnance Map: Stoke-on-Trent and Macclesfield area: Sheet 118:
1/50,000
Map Ref: SJ 670/693
Access: On east side of A.533 Northwich-Middlewich road, opposite
recreation ground.

This large oak tree, standing in its railed enclosure, is traditionally considered to mark the exact centre of the county of Cheshire. By what

Oak at centre of Cheshire, Bostock Green.

calculation the spot was arrived at has never been explained, though.

There was an "ancient oak" standing on this spot in the middle of the last century, but by the 1880s it had become unsafe and a potential danger to passers-by. Queen Victoria's Golden Jubilee in 1887 provided an opportunity to cut it down and plant a successor, the present tree.

One of the two plaques at the tree's foot includes the puzzling words "planted by Rev. Canon Col. and Cap. Hayhurst". The solution is that Canon, Colonel and Captain were father, son and grandson, and not one individual.

If you want to be absolutely sure of having stood at the centre of Cheshire, a visit to Davenham Church is recommended. Its spire, prominent a mile or so to the north of Bostock, is the only other contender for the title, though again, evidence to back its claim seems to be lacking.

Places of Interest in the Neighbourhood
52. Imprisoned Below Stairs? (Over)
65. A Famous Foxhound (Sandiway)
76. Birthplace of the Cheshire Prophet (Whitegate)

School Farm (former Bradwall reformatory), Bradwall Green. Note original central doorway allowing passage of horse-drawn wagons into central courtyard.

16 Farming in a Former Reformatory

Position: Bradwall Green, 2 miles north of Sandbach
Ordnance Map: Stoke-on-Trent and Macclesfield area; Sheet 118;
1/50,000
Map Ref: SJ 755/639
Access: School Farm and School Cottages stand on the north side of
Walnut Tree Lane.

Bradwall Reformatory School was founded in 1855 by the local landowner, George William Latham of Bradwall Hall. Funds also came
from neighbouring nobility and gentry, plus a Government grant. The
aim was to take boys from the Sandbach area who had got into trouble
with the law, and to teach them agricultural skills in order to keep them
from drifting into a life of crime.

The cost of building the school, which had forty acres of land in
addition to the farm buildings, was £255. 10s. 2d. Forty boys were
taught by a general superintendent and four other masters. As well as
being taught draining, hedging, ditching and so on, the boys received
three hours education each day.

In 1880 the reformatory was enlarged and a cottage hospital added.
Under the later title of Sandbach Training School, the establishment
continued in its role until after the First World War.

It is to be hoped that the sentiments expressed in White's *Cheshire
Directory* of 1860 were realised: " . . . we doubt not but that in after
years many there are who will look with a grateful eye on the originator
of the institution as being the instrument of redeeming them from a
life of crime and wickedness to one of sobriety, industry and morality,
and raising them to a station in life unattainable but for the good will
and kindness of the benevolent and esteemed founder of the Bradwall
Reformatory School."

Places of Interest in the Neighbourhood
23. A Railway Timekeeper (Crewe)
24. The Value of Time (Crewe Green)
64. Saxon Sculpture Smashed and Reassembled (Sandbach)

17 The Poacher's Revenge

Position: Bunbury
Ordnance Map: Chester, Wrexham and surrounding area: Sheet 117: 1/50,000
Map Ref: SJ 558/585
Access: On west side of the A.49 road.

The Image House would be an undistinguished nineteenth century cottage were it not for the carved heads which can be seen on and around the building.

It is said to have been one of those buildings "built in a night". In former times, if a person could build a house on a piece of common land between sunset and sunrise, he was reckoned to acquire right of residence. This concept never formed part of the law of the land, but seems to have been generally accepted. In practice, it seems to have been sufficient to have had the chimney smoking by dawn, and the rest of the house could then be constructed at leisure. This must have been the case here, if the story has any truth in it.

The builder of this particular cottage is said to have been a local poacher who was sentenced to transportation for his crimes in the early nineteenth century. On his return to his native soil, he built the Image House and decorated its exterior with rough likenesses of the men – gamekeepers, constables, justices and so on – who had been responsible for his fate. His aim was obviously to invoke some magical power to cause them harm. The story is told by Beatrice Tunstall in her novel *The Shiny Night*, in which the poacher is given the name Seth Shone.

Places of Interest in the Neighbourhood
19. The Round House (Chorley)
28. The Copper Mine Chimney (Gallantry Bank)
55. The Elephant and Castle (Peckforton)

Image House, Whitchurch Road, Bunbury.

18 One Hand on the Clock – Two Graves in the Wood

Position: Burton, off the A.540 between Chester and Neston
Ordnance Map: Chester, Wrexham and surrounding area: Sheet 117: 1/50,000
Map Ref: SJ 317/743
Access: Burton Parish Church is on the north side of the road which runs through the village.

The church's dedication to St. Nicholas, patron saint of sailors, indicates that Burton, like most villages on this side of the Wirral peninsula, had maritime connections before silting destroyed the trade of the River Dee. Most of the fabric now visible dates from 1721, and the clock,

Church of St Nicholas, Burton (note one-handed clock).

Quakers' graves, Burton.

notable for its having an hour hand but no minute hand, was added to the tower in 1751. It was the work of Joseph Smith of Chester, and must have been a late example of this type of clock; there are apparently only about a dozen one-handed church clocks surviving in the whole of the country. It seems that visitors often have trouble in telling the time by this one until they are given instruction by a local!

If you cross the graveyard to the left of the church and go up some sandstone steps at the rear, you will find yourself in a wood. The path soon forks; take the left fork and in about 50 metres you will find two gravestone slabs enclosed by a low rail on the right of the path. The inscriptions, now indecipherable, were still partly visible in 1877 when they were recorded, the date on one of them appearing as 1663.

Long-standing local tradition refers to them as the "Quaker Graves", and says that a man and wife were buried there. While it is certain that the graves represent deliberate burials outside consecrated ground, the identity of their occupants remains unknown, and there is no historical evidence for any presence of Quakerism in Burton during the period in question. The graves, therefore, remain something of a mystery.

From this point, you can either return to the road by the way you came, or continue along the path for about another 200 metres to a track junction, turn left, and regain the road that way.

Places of Interest in the Neighbourhood
67. Where Irishmen Hung in Irons (Saughall)
68. Cheshire's Gretna Green (Shotwick)
77. Just the Place to Catch the Ghost Train (Willaston)

19 The Round House

Position: Chorley, near Nantwich
Ordnance Map: Chester, Wrexham and surrounding area: Sheet 117:
1/50,000
Map Ref: SJ 574/510
Access: On south side of unclassified road, east of telephone box.

Why call an octagonal building "The Round House"? The answer is
that "round house" was a term formerly used for a lock-up, apparently
regardless of the building's shape. This late 18th century structure, now
a private house, started life as the village bridewell. The rooms inside
radiate from the centre. What seems surprising is first of all the large
size of the building compared to most village lock-ups, and secondly its
isolated position. Perhaps there was more crime in these parts than one
imagines!

Places of Interest in the Neighbourhood
  1. The End of the Game? (Acton)
28. The Copper Mine Chimney (Gallantry Bank)
47. A Sacrifice Still Remembered (Nantwich)

The Round House (former Bridewell), Chorley.

20 A Zoo in the Basement

Position: Christleton, south-east of Chester
Ordnance Map: Chester, Wrexham and surrounding area: Sheet 117:
1/50,000
Map Ref: SJ 441/656
Access: In centre of village, around the green.

About two-thirds of the way up the path between the lych-gate and
the church of St. James, on the right-hand side, is the pink sandstone
upright slab which marks the grave of William Huggins.

The epitaph on his tombstone fulsomely describes him as "an Historic
and Animal Painter of acknowledged eminence" and "A just and com-
passionate man who would neither tread on a worm nor cringe to an
emperor".

Huggins was born in Liverpool in 1820 and at the age of 15 won a
prize at the Mechanics' Institute for a painting of an historical subject.
Later he turned to the drawing and painting of animals for which he is
best remembered today, though in fact he was extremely versatile. He
exhibited at the Royal Academy between 1846 and 1875.

After living in Chester and North Wales, he moved to Christleton in
1880, and resided at Rock House, which can be seen beside the village
green, south of the church. By this time he was suffering from arthritis
and virtually retired, though he still painted and drew when he felt well
enough. Here he died peacefully on 25th February, 1884.

Two local traditions concerning him are recorded, though how true
they are is hard to say. One is that he kept wild animals in the cellars of
Rock House, so that he could draw them from life, and the other is that
he composed his epitaph himself.

Places of Interest in the Neighbourhood
21. The Winning Post (Christleton)
36. Where Packhorses Plodded (Hockenhull Platts)
71. The Incomparable Penman (Tarvin)

21 The Winning Post

Position: Christleton, south-east of Chester
Ordnance Map: Chester, Wrexham and surrounding area: Sheet 117:
1/50,000
Map Ref: SJ 440/651
Access: On west side of A.41 road.

In the days when the A.41 was even narrower and more winding than it
is now, motorists driving to Chester from the West Midlands came to
look upon this structure as a kind of "winning post" indicating that
their journey was nearly at an end, for hereabouts the outskirts of the
city begin.

They were probably unaware of the "winning post's" purpose. The
hexagonal part at the top, with its pyramidal roof, looks as though it
might be some sort of dovecote, but why is it perched on such a tall
cast-iron column?

Messrs. Adams of York, who installed it around 1900, knew. The
"dovecote" contains a pump and header tank; the whole thing is a
hydraulic sewage lift, providing pressure to force Christleton's sewage
over a rise in the ground here, and into the Chester City system.

The lift is no longer in use, but has become such a local landmark that
it is maintained in good repair, in spite of its having been unkindly
described as an "outsize lavatory flush."

Places of Interest in the Neighbourhood
20. A Zoo in the Basement (Christleton)
36. Where Packhorses Plodded (Hockenhull Platts)
71. The Incomparable Penman (Tarvin)

Sewage Lift, Christleton.

22 Hot Jewellery

Position: Clutton, on the A.534 road approximately 1 mile west of its intersection with the A.41 at Broxton
Ordnance Map: Chester, Wrexham and surrounding area: Sheet 117: 1/50,000
Map Ref: SJ 461/544
Access: On the south side of the A.534 just west of Clutton village.

The two baroque lodges, which now look rather out of place beside the road, date from about 1830. The one on the right as viewed from the road was the lodge-keeper's day quarters and the one on the left was where he slept. Both have fireplaces, and the urn finial on the top of each domed roof also serves as a chimney. The railings are early 18th century work by the Davies Brothers of Croes Foel, Wrexham, who carried out wrought iron work at many of the great houses of the Welsh border; they were also responsible for the original gates, which have gone, the present ones being replacements.

This rather delightful ensemble was formerly the north entrance to Carden Park. All that remains of the mansion are the stables and other outbuildings just visible through the gates. The house itself, a large half-timbered Jacobean edifice, was destroyed by fire on the night of 16th September, 1912. At that time it was tenanted by Colonel George Holdsworth who, with his wife, maintained the old style of country house hospitality, and in fact, a house party was in progress at the time.

About 3.30 a.m. one of the lady guests heard a noise which she thought was burglars. She woke her host's daughter, who woke the Colonel, and it was he who discovered the fire. He telephoned for the local fire brigades, which arrived from Farndon, Broxton, Malpas and Chester in that order. But the house was doomed even before the firemen arrived.

Before the party had retired the previous night, the jewellery belonging to the ladies, especially Mrs. Holdsworth and Lady Worsley, had been put in the safe. The firemen found this among the debris and it was dragged out on to the lawn with the aid of ropes. Unfortunately, its door was open – it was said that either Mrs. Holdsworth or her maid had attempted to save the valuables before fleeing the burning building, and had got the safe door open, but then been beaten back by smoke.

The contents of the safe were spread into a big shallow box lined with newspaper, and the firemen, policemen and helpers from neighbouring farms were then treated to the spectacle of a number of ladies of quality

Clutton Lodge (to Carden Park).

on their knees on the grass scrabbling about trying to pick out what they could from the charred mass. The gold was completely melted and the pearls were black, but some diamonds and rubies were saved. Had the safe been locked, the probability is that the contents would have survived intact.

A mile due south stands the park's southern entrance, Carden Lodge (Map Ref. SJ 461/528). This is in the form of a huge classical triumphal arch, a complete contrast in style to the rather jolly Clutton Lodge.

Places of Interest in the Neighbourhood
12. The Best of British Castramentation (Bickerton)
26. Recalling the Relief of Lucknow (Farndon)
27. The Roundheads' Gateway to Wales (Farndon)
74. No Shelter for the Mourners Here (Tilston)

23　A Railway Timekeeper

Position: Crewe
Ordnance Map: Stoke-on-Trent & Macclesfield area: Sheet 118:
1/50,000
Map Ref: SJ 687/557
Access: In Queen's Park, on the south side of Victoria Avenue.

Ever since Crewe mushroomed out of the sparsely populated township of Monks Coppenhall in the 1840s, it has been impossible to mention the town's name without thinking of the railway which gave it birth and on which it depended for its livelihood.

For over a century the railway dominated the town, via the rail traffic represented by the vast station and the engineering industry represented by the famous locomotive works situated on the opposite side of Victoria Avenue to Queen's Park.

The clock tower in the park was donated by employees of the London and North Western Railway Company to commemorate Queen Victoria's Golden Jubilee of 1887, and erected the following year. It is possible to read a variety of meanings into the structure, if so inclined.

The four-faced clock can obviously be taken to represent the importance of good timekeeping to the efficient operation of the railway. Look next at the heads contained in the finials above the triangular panels on the four sides of the tower. That to the north is Queen Victoria herself; the other three are members of the board of the L.N.W.R. Co. In the eyes of the railwaymen, they were perhaps of equal importance to the Queen, in Crewe at least.

And why is Victoria given the view of the loco works, while the railway magnates turn their gaze elsewhere? Was it because the donors of the tower wanted to make her see the basis of Crewe's prosperity?

Places of Interest in the Neighbourhood

Clock Tower, Queen's Park, Crewe.

24 The Value of Time

Position: Crewe Green, east of Crewe
Ordnance Map: Stoke-on-Trent & Macclesfield area: Sheet 118:
1/50,000
Map Ref: SJ 727/554
Access: On the north side of the Crewe-Haslington road, opposite the church.

The village hall here was originally the local school, and the centre of the south wall was evidently designed to make a forcible impression on the pupils. Starting at the top, we see a sundial with an inscription below it reading "Use Well Thy Time". Further down the wall is another inscription: "What Shall We Render Unto the Lord".

Still lower comes the culmination. This is set into the wall above yet another inscription, reading "Time Rewarding Industry And Punishing Sloth". The finely sculptured panel depicts the winged figure of Time. In one hand he holds a whip, with which he menaces an idle lad in rags, among weeds by a neglected house. With the other he presents a laurel wreath to an industrious boy with a spade.

Places of Interest in the Neighbourhood
23. A Railway Timekeeper (Crewe)
64. Saxon Sculpture Smashed and Reassembled (Sandbach)
80. The Time and the Inclination (Wybunbury)

Village Hall (former school), Crewe Green.

25 Birthplace of Wonderland's Creator

Position: Daresbury
Ordnance Map: Liverpool and surrounding area: Sheet 108: 1/50,000
Map Ref: SJ 593/805
Access: The plaque marking the site stands in a wooden railed enclosure on the south-west side of Morphany Lane.

On 27th January 1832, at Daresbury Parsonage, was born Charles Lutwidge Dodson, better known as Lewis Carroll, author of *Alice's Adventures in Wonderland.*

Unfortunately for his admirers, the Parsonage was destroyed by fire in 1883, and all that remains of it today is a well-head. The plaque marking the site was placed there by the local Lewis Carroll society.

Daresbury church, one and a half miles to the north-west, contains a memorial window depicting characters from *Alice*, based on the well-known Tenniel illustrations. Near the church stands the former Sessions House, and the Lewis Carroll Birthplace Trust intends to transform this and the adjoining barn and stable block into a Lewis Carroll Centre. Look for the weathervane on the village school, too!

Places of Interest in the Neighbourhood
  7. Bawming the Thorn (Appleton)
34. For Future Service or Recollection (Halton)
70. "Time Is Not All" (Stretton)

Plaque marking site of Daresbury Parsonage.

26 Recalling the Relief of Lucknow

Position: Farndon
Ordnance Map: Chester, Wrexham and surrounding area: Sheet 117:
1/50,000
Map Ref: SJ 413/551
Access: On the west side of Churton Road, the unclassified road
between Churton and Farndon.

This tall slender needle commemorates Major Roger Barnston of the
90th Light Infantry, a member of a prominent family living at Crewe
Hill nearby. He served in both the Crimean War and the Indian
Mutiny. While leading an assault at the relief of Lucknow on 16th
November 1857 he received a severe wound, from the effects of which
he died at Cawnpore on 23rd December, and was buried there. He was
31 years of age.

A public subscription for a memorial was raised locally, and his
brother William offered a premium for the best design. The prize went
to Mr. E.A. Heffer, and the monument was made from stone from the
Cefn quarries in North Wales. Its total height is 55 feet, the length of
the needle itself being 40 feet. The cost was £400.

Places of Interest in the Neighbourhood
 3. An Original "Telford" (Aldford)
 4. The Duke's Dispensary (Aldford)
27. The Roundheads' Gateway to Wales (Farndon)

Barnston Memorial, Farndon.

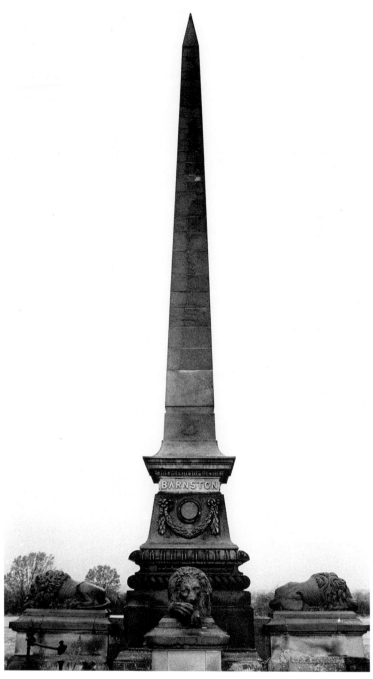

47

27 The Roundheads' Gateway to Wales

Position: Farndon
Ordnance Map: Chester, Wrexham & surrounding area: Sheet 117: 1/50,000
Map Ref: SJ 412/544
Access: From the south-west end of High Street.

This fine eight-arched sandstone bridge probably dates from the fourteenth century. In 1778, Thomas Pennant recorded that "the date, 1345, was preserved, till very lately, on a stone over the arch called the Lady's arch." This statement seems rather dubious, but documentary evidence does suggest a date between 1315 and 1397 for the bridge's origin.

The "Lady's arch" is the third one from the Welsh side, the one which has an additional arch-ring above the main one. This is probably

Farndon Bridge.

the span which, during the Civil War, was fortified by the Welsh Royalists. They erected a guardhouse, with a drawbridge and gates, when Parliamentary forces under the command of Sir William Brereton were attempting to force a passage of the River Dee upstream of Chester, to which they had laid siege.

On 7th December 1643, Brereton commenced a decoy river-crossing operation a mile downstream of Farndon. This feint succeeded in drawing the Royalist infantry away from the bridge, and, as Brereton reported to Parliament "gave us the opportunity to make a desperate assault upon the bridge by placing ladders to the toppe of the drawbridge and cutting the ropes. Which being done and the bridge falling down wee had accesse to the gates and casting over some hand granadoes amongst the Welshmen – who there remayned – which struck such terror into them as that they all run away and could not be obtained to relieve. Whereby wee had a verie faire opportunity to force open the gates: which being done the enimy was without much difficultie beaten from theire double workes within the gates . . . "

This brisk skirmish opened the way into North Wales for the Parliamentary forces and was an important factor in forcing the eventual surrender of Chester.

Places of Interest in the Neighbourhood
  3. An Original "Telford" (Aldford)
  4. The Duke's Dispensary (Aldford)
26. Recalling the Relief of Lucknow (Farndon)

28 The Copper Mine Chimney

Position: Gallantry Bank, near Bickerton
Ordnance Map: Chester, Wrexham and surrounding area: Sheet 117:
1/50,000
Map Ref: SJ 517/542
Access: Coppermine Lane is on the north side of the A.534
approximately 2 miles east of its intersection with the A.41 at Broxton.
Parking on south side of road opposite.

The earliest reference to copper mines in Cheshire dates from 1670, and
although no names are mentioned, it is likely that this mine at Bickerton was in existence then. It was certainly being worked in 1690, and an
agreement drawn up in that year mentions pits already excavated on the
site. "Gallantry Bank", the hill on whose slopes the mine stood, was
originally Gallows-tree Bank, so called because the body of a murderer
named Holford was gibbetted there in 1640.

   The mine was worked intermittently over the next two centuries. The
probability is that it was never more than marginally viable in economic
terms, and so it would only have been profitable to work it when copper
was fetching a good price. On occasion outside experts would be
brought in to report on the mine's possibilities, and their origins
demonstrate where mining skills were considered to lie in their respec-
tive periods. In 1697, for example, J.D. Brandshagen, a German, made
suggestions regarding layout of the workings, assayed the ore and drew
up rules for miners. Just over a century later, another assessment was
made by Captain Thomas Dunstan, an experienced Cornish miner who
came up from Falmouth in 1806.

   Such visits and reports would herald a phase of activity, eventually
followed by a period of closure. The final mining operations took place
in the 1920s, when three local men carried out small scale working for a
number of years. Then, in the winter of 1928-29 the mine buildings were
demolished, the shafts were later sealed or filled in, and now all that
remains to the non-expert eye is the red sandstone chimney stack, constructed in 1856, an isolated reminder of men's efforts to win wealth
from the earth.

Places of Interest in the Neighbourhood
12. The Best of British Castramentation (Bickerton)
17. The Poacher's Revenge (Bunbury)
55. The Elephant and Castle (Peckforton)

Copper mine chimney, Gallantry Bank, Bickerton.

29 "Old Maggoty" or "Lord Flame"?

Position: Gawsworth, south-east of Macclesfield
Ordnance Map: Stoke-on-Trent and Macclesfield area: Sheet 118:
1/50,000
Map Ref: SJ 888/702
Access: Maggotty's Wood lies on the north side of Maggotty Lane,
which runs eastward between the A.536 Macclesfield-Congleton road
and Church Lane.

No lexicographer was the Cheshire Samuel Johnson. Born somewhere
in the county in 1691, he earned his early living as a dancing-master to
local gentry families. His gifts as a wit, poet, musician and actor took
him to London, where his play *Hurlothrumbo, or the Supernatural*, in
which he acted the part of Lord Flame, made him one of the chief topics
of talk in 1729. He wrote numerous other works, some of which were
never published, but he never repeated his early meteoric success, and in
later years he lived on subsidies from wealthy patrons.

   In the early 1740s he came to live in part of the New Hall at
Gawsworth, by the kindness of the Earl of Harrington, to whose family
he had formerly acted as dancing-master. His brief fame had apparently
gone to his head, for he came to think of himself as really being Lord
Flame, and, to humour him, his patrons used to send their contribu-
tions to the Earl's steward, who would accumulate them and, once a
year, wait upon Johnson with the words, "My Lord, I have brought you
your rents." "Lord Flame" would then issue a formal receipt. The local
rustics, too, used to address him as "My Lord" to his face, but behind
his back as "Old Maggoty", a term signifying whimsical, capricious, or
crotchety.

   His wit brought him into great demand at the houses of the local
gentry, and his later life may be said to have been spent as one of the
last professional jesters in England. Before his death, he had expressed
his desire to be buried in the little wood where he had loved to walk in
his last years. The reason he gave, as expressed in his epitaph, was

> That when he rose again, laid here alone,
> No friend and he should quarrel for a bone;
> Thinking that were some old lame gossip nigh,
> She possibly might take his leg or thigh.

   While this brand of humour no doubt went down well at the time of
his death in 1773, it was not so well received by the Victorians, and so

Maggotty Johnson's grave, Gawsworth.

in 1851 Lady Harrington had the local curate, the Reverend Edward Massie, compose some admonitory verses which were engraved on a slab placed alongside Maggoty's tomb as an antidote.

When the Gawsworth estate was sold in 1920, the new owner of the wood restored the brick tomb-chest, re-lettered the inscriptions, and gave the site to the National Trust.

To reach the tomb from the junction of Maggotty Lane and Church Lane, enter the wood and follow the path which leads to the right up the hill. You will find Maggoty's – or Lord Flame's – grave at the top. His ghost has long been said to haunt the area.

Places of Interest in the Neighbourhood
30. Where the Dark Lady Walks (Gawsworth)
33. Where the Schemer Learned His Trade (Gurnett)
35. The Village that Fell Asleep (Havannah)
45. Six Centuries of Worship (Marton)

53

30 Where the Dark Lady Walks

Position: Gawsworth, south-west of Macclesfield
Ordnance Map: Stoke-on-Trent & Macclesfield area: Sheet 118:
1/50,000
Map Ref: SJ 887/695
Access: This section of Church Lane runs south-west from the church.

This fine avenue of seventy-four lime trees was planted in 1827. Apart from its natural attractiveness, it is also claimed to be one of the places where the ghost of Mary Fitton walks. Mary, baptised here on 24th June, 1578, was a daughter of the Fitton family, Lords of the Manor of Gawsworth. At the age of seventeen she became a maid of honour to Queen Elizabeth I, a position from which she was dismissed in 1601 when she was found to be pregnant by William Herbert, who later became Earl of Pembroke. She is also said to have had two more illegitimate children by Sir Richard Leveson at a later date. Her first husband was Captain William Polwhele, whom she married about 1606. After his death in 1610, Mary married Captain John Lougher. He died about 1635, but Mary lived on until 1647.

She has been identified, on rather slender evidence, with the "Dark Lady" of Shakespeare's sonnets.

In her will she directed that she should be interred at Gawsworth, though no record of her burial here exists. Other members of the family are interred in the church, where their monuments can be seen, including one in which Mary herself is represented. Her ghost has been reported in both the lime avenue and the church.

Places of Interest in the Neighbourhood
29. "Old Maggoty" or "Lord Flame"? (Gawsworth)
33. Where the Schemer Learned His Trade (Gurnett)
35. The Village that Fell Asleep (Havannah)
45. Six Centuries of Worship (Marton)

31 Water with Some Body to It

Position: Great Budworth, 2 miles north of Northwich
Ordnance Map: Stoke-on-Trent and Macclesfield area: Sheet 118:
1/50,000
Map Ref: SJ 662/774
Access: At south-east side of intersection of A.559 and unclassified
road. Parking in Great Budworth village.

Dene Well-house was erected in 1880 to the design of Edmund Kirby
(perhaps better known for his churches) and at the expense of either
Rowland Egerton Warburton of Arley Hall or his son Piers. It was

Dene Well-house, Great Budworth.

Rowland who was responsible for the verse above the flowing spout:

> Blessings in never ending love
> Are on us poured from Heaven above.
> This running stream with ceaseless flow
> Springs from the bounteous earth below;
> Alike in both His goodness shown
> Whom heaven and earth their maker own.

The well was the local source of drinking water until a piped supply was introduced in 1934. At one point the water was found to be rather highly flavoured, a phenomenon which persisted until investigation of the "bounteous earth" of the slope behind the well-house revealed that the "running stream" had been contaminated by that traditionally uncommon sight, a dead donkey.

Places of Interest in the Neighbourhood
  6. Unique in this Country – First in the World (Anderton)
  8. Rhymes of a Fox Hunting Man (Arley)
 50. It Floats! It Swings!! It's Electric!!! (Northwich)

32 Contrasting Faces of a Baptist Chapel

Position: Great Warford, between Alderley Edge and Knutsford
Ordnance Map: Stoke-on-Trent & Macclesfield area: Sheet 118: 1/50,000
Map Ref: SJ 816/770
Access: On the north side of Merryman's Lane.

The congregation which founded this chapel probably owed its origins to the strongly Puritan element among the Parliamentary soldiers who were stationed in this part of Cheshire during the Civil War. In 1668 some of these men, or their spiritual successors, met together for worship in a local farmhouse. This secret meeting-room was vacated soon afterwards in favour of a more suitable one in Pownall Brow Farm, about a mile to the north of the present chapel.

Eventually, the number of worshippers grew too large for the room, and since Dissenting chapels could now be licensed under the Toleration Act, an ancient barn and adjoining cottage were acquired in 1712 and converted into the chapel building which we see today.

The south side, visible from the road, looks as unremarkable as most Dissenting places of worship of the period, but when the conversion was carried out the north side was left untouched, and what we see is basically an early Tudor barn, except that the original wattle and daub between the massive oak frames has been replaced by brick.

The chapel originally occupied the whole of the building, but it was later divided into two portions, of which the eastern is retained for worship. All the furniture in this part is original.

Places of Interest in the Neighbourhood
 2. The Wizard and Mr. Garner (Alderley Edge)
49. An Elizabethan Corn Mill (Nether Alderley)
78. Romany's Garden of Remembrance (Wilmslow)

33 Where the Schemer Learned His Trade

Position: Gurnett, near Macclesfield
Ordnance Map: Stoke-on-Trent and Macclesfield area: Sheet 118:
1/50,000
Map Ref: SJ 926/717
Access: Plough House is on the north side of Byron's Lane,
approximately 100 yards east of the Macclesfield Canal aqueduct.

James Brindley (1716-1772), the pioneer of Britain's canal system, was
born near Buxton in Derbyshire, but it was here that he came at the age
of seventeen to serve his apprenticeship as a millwright. A plaque on the
garage of Plough House records that:

ON THESE PREMISES
1733-1740
JAMES BRINDLEY
THE FAMOUS CIVIL ENGINEER
AND CANAL BUILDER, SERVED
AS APPRENTICE TO ABRAHAM
BENNETT.

Bennett seems to have been fonder of the tavern than the millwright's
shop, and Brindley does not seem to have made much progress during
the early part of his apprenticeship. In fact he gained the reputation of a
botcher of jobs and spoiler of materials.

The breakthrough came when Bennett was given the job of installing
the machinery in a new mill about five miles away. The waterwheel and
gearing at Folly Mill were intended to be like those at Smedley Mill in
Manchester. Bennett noted the details of the latter and tried to
reproduce them at Folly Mill, but to no avail. The machinery would not
fit or run, in spite of prolonged effort by Bennett and his workforce,
including young Brindley.

Then one Saturday Brindley vanished. Everyone assumed that he had
simply broken his indentures and run off. But on the Monday morning
he was back at work as usual. On the Saturday night he had walked to
Manchester, a distance of over twenty miles. Sunday had been spent
memorising the details of Smedley Mill's machinery, with the owner's
permission, and that night he had walked back to his workplace.

Bennett, in desperation perhaps, gave him a free hand, and Brindley
had Folly Mill fully operational in a matter of weeks.

Thereafter, Brindley was given complete charge of his master's shop,

James Brindley (from Samuel Smiles Lives of the Engineers).

and when Bennett died a few years later, Brindley kept it going until all contracts were completed before setting up his own business near Leek in Staffordshire.

Brindley had memorised the workings of Smedley Mill because all through his life he had great difficulty with reading and writing. His way of solving problems did not involve pencil and paper. He acquired the nickname of "the schemer" because of his habit of retiring somewhere quiet (even staying in bed for days at a time) until he had every detail of a project worked out in his head.

Places of Interest in the Neighbourhood
29. "Old Maggoty" or "Lord Flame" (Gawsworth)
30. Where the Dark Lady Walks (Gawsworth)
35. The Village that Fell Asleep (Havannah)

34 For Future Service or Recollection

Position: Halton, Runcorn
Ordnance Map: Liverpool & surrounding area: Sheet 108: 1/50,000
Map Ref: SJ 537/818
Access: Sir John Chesshyre's Library is on the west side of Castle Road.

This building, which now serves as a committee room for the adjoining church hall, was originally the home of one of the earliest free village libraries in the country. It was built in 1730 at the expense of Sir John Chesshyre of Hallwood nearby, although it was not finally fitted out until 1733, the date recorded in the inscription over the original entrance.

Sir John provided a stock of some 500 volumes. The original rules of the library provided that "any divine or divines of the Church of England, or other gentlemen, or persons of letters could, on application to the curate, use the library in the daytime on any Tuesday, and take notes from the books therein." Sir John had no intention of excluding women readers, for the taking of notes by a reader was "for his, her, or their future service or recollection."

Although free, it was not really a public library in any normal sense. The titles represented were overwhelmingly theological, and a later writer went so far as to say that "it would probably be difficult to select five hundred volumes that would present fewer attractions to the villagers of Halton."

The interior of the building has been completely altered from its original form, and Sir John's volumes no longer line its walls. The inscription remains, however, to recall his undoubtedly kind intentions.

Places of Interest in the Neighbourhood
   7. Bawming the Thorn (Appleton)
25. Birthplace of Wonderland's Creator (Daresbury)
70. "Time Is Not All" (Stretton)

35 The Village that Fell Asleep

Position: Havannah, 1 mile north-east of Congleton
Ordnance Map: Stoke-on-Trent and Macclesfield area: Sheet 118:
1/50,000
Map Ref: SJ 870/646
Access: East of the A.536 Congleton – Macclesfield road. Havannah
Lane, the unsurfaced road which is the only route for vehicles, is not a
public right of way.

The story of this remote industrial community really begins when
Charles Roe, who introduced silk to Macclesfield, branched out into
copper smelting in that town in 1758. He was soon looking for additional premises, and in 1763 he leased some land by the River Dane in
Eaton, where he could use the river to provide water-power for his
works. These he named Havannah in commemoration of the capture of
the Cuban capital by British forces in the previous year. As well as the
works, seven cottages were constructed. Brass and copper wire and
sheets were produced here until the early years of the nineteenth
century, when demand declined and parts of the premises were used for
cotton spinning and corn grinding. After the Napoleonic Wars corn and
silk mills were established, the latter lasting until about 1860, and more
cottages were built for the workers.

Towards the end of last century a tobacco firm set up in the former
silk mill, manufacturing "genuine Havannah cigars". The ploy was
successful, for not many years afterwards they moved to larger premises
in the centre of Congleton.

Then began the "big sleep". Before long, brambles snaked out of the
windows of the cottages, grass grew knee-high on the pavement, and
moss choked the cobbled street. In the years before the First World War
the deserted village achieved local notoriety, and visitors to Congleton
would often come out for a look at it.

This state of affairs lasted until 1920, when a velvet cutting firm,
whose lease on its Warrington factory was running out, took over the
two disused silk mills. The velvet cutters, too, have now gone (the trade
ended in 1958), but Havannah, though still remote, is now firmly awake
again.

Places of Interest in the Neighbourhood
29. "Old Maggoty" or "Lord Flame" (Gawsworth)
30. Where the Dark Lady Walks (Gawsworth)

36 Where Packhorses Plodded

Position: Hockenhull Platts, 1 mile south-west of Tarvin
Ordnance Map: Chester, Wrexham and surrounding area: Sheet 117:
1/50,000
Map Ref: SJ 476/657
Access: The best approach is on foot from Sheaf Farm (Map Ref. SJ
490/654). A shorter alternative (though less atmospheric) is from the
unclassified road to the east, along which cars can be taken as far as the
junction with the Cotton Farm drive (Map Ref. SJ 472/656).

From the crossways by Sheaf Farm, take the narrow surfaced track
which runs westwards past the farmhouse. In a little over half a mile the
Baker Way (a waymarked walkers' route) comes in from the north and
the route then narrows and becomes a gravel footpath. Another quarter
of a mile brings you rather unexpectedly to the first (easternmost) of the
three packhorse bridges over the River Gowy and its feeders, and the

Central Packhorse bridge, Hockenhull Platts.

narrow cobbled road which crosses them.

Incredible though it seems, the narrow way along which you have come was once the main road from London to Chester.

Although referred to locally as the "Roman Bridges", they are in fact medieval in origin. In August 1353 the Black Prince, as Earl of Chester, made a state visit to Cheshire, travelling from Staffordshire to Chester by a route which was the ancestor of the present A.51 road. The following month, among other gifts for local charitable purposes, he granted twenty shillings "for the repair of the bridge at Hockenhull", the implication being that he had travelled over it earlier.

A petition for a collection to cover the cost of repairs was made in 1614, and further work was undertaken in the eighteenth century – it is this which can be seen in the fabric of the present bridges. They were never wide enough even for carts, and by the mid-seventeenth century alternative routes to north and south were being used by wheeled traffic.

This is still, however, the most direct route between Tarporley and Chester, and proposals to drive a modern highway through have been made at various times. Fortunately, nothing has come of any of them, and so it is still possible to get the feeling here of traversing a stretch of medieval roadway, perhaps as part of the Black Prince's retinue.

A good spot for a rest or picnic before returning to Sheaf Farm can be found by turning left on to the river bank after crossing the second bridge. Signs hereabouts point out that Hockenhull Platts is a nature reserve, so please be particularly careful to respect the environment.

Places of Interest in the Neighbourhood
20. A Zoo in the Basement (Christleton)
21. The Winning Post (Christleton)
71. The Incomparable Penman (Tarvin)

37 Searching the Skies

Position: Jodrell Bank, north-east of Holmes Chapel
Ordnance Map: Stoke-on-Trent & Macclesfield area: Sheet 118:
1/50,000
Map Ref: SJ 795/711
Access: The telescope is situated west of the A.535 Holmes Chapel –
Alderley Edge road. It is visible for miles around – simply steer towards
it and follow signs as you get closer. If you wish to know more about the
functioning of the telescope, the Science Centre on the site describes all
this and much more: check times and charges.

The decision to site the huge Mark 1A radio telescope here was
taken simply because there was too much electrical interference in
Manchester. This prevented efficient operation there of the ex-Army
radar sets with which radio astronomy began at the end of the Second
World War. Manchester University had a botanical research station at
Jodrell Bank, and Bernard Lovell (later Sir Bernard), then a lecturer
in physics, obtained permission to set up his radar equipment there
towards the end of 1945.

The telescope was five years in the building, from 1952 to 1957.
Originally called the Mark 1, its designation was altered after improve-
ments in 1970-71. The period of its construction was beset with dif-
ficulties over funding, but providentially its completion coincided with
the launching of the first artificial earth satellite (the Soviet Sputnik I).
It was used to track this and the later Soviet and American satellites,
thus achieving immediate media attention, which brought this formerly
little-known part of Cheshire into the international limelight, which it
still enjoys for its prominence in radio astronomy.

Places of Interest in the Neighbourhood
42. Weightlifting for Would-be Wives (Lower Peover)
45. Six Centuries of Worship (Marton)
53. Where "Old Blood and Guts" had His Headquarters (Over Peover)

38 Narrow Pavements – and Watt Architecture!

Position: Knutsford
Ordnance Map: Stoke-on-Trent & Macclesfield area: Sheet 118: 1/50,000
Map Ref: SJ 753/785
Access: This short walk starts from the bottom of King Street, near the railway station.

Begin by walking up King Street. Ahead of you, on the left-hand side you will see a tall white square tower, your first introduction to the eccentric architecture which is Knutsford's legacy from that equally eccentric character Richard Harding Watt.

Watt was a wealthy Manchester glove manufacturer who took up residence in Knutsford towards the end of the last century. His architectural inspiration can best be summarised as Mediterranean, drawing as it does chiefly on Italian and Islamic sources. He employed architects for his projects, but seems to have regarded them as little more than draughtsmen employed to translate his ideas into practice.

The tower was built in 1907 as Watt's tribute to Mrs. Elizabeth Gaskell, the novelist who spent her formative years here and brought Knutsford to literary life as "Cranford". On the face of the tower can be seen a bust of Mrs. Gaskell and a list of her principal works, as well as other carved details.

The adjoining building, crowned by a dome, is the King's Coffee House (now a restaurant), which he originally intended as a cultural centre serving non-alcoholic drinks for the benefit of the townspeople.

Continuing up King Street, notice the narrowness of the pavement on the left-hand side. This was originally the only pavement in the street, and the cost of laying it was borne by Lady Jane Stanley towards the end of the eighteenth century. She bequeathed £400 for its subsequent upkeep, on condition that it should be no more than one paving-stone wide. The reason, apparently, was that she had a strong aversion to the sight of couples walking arm-in-arm.

After passing the Post Office at the top of the street (note the sundial over the door), turn right into Drury Lane. Immediately, you are confronted with another of Watt's oddities, the Ruskin Rooms. Named after his favourite poet, it combines Italianate, Moorish and Art Nouveau features, and was built around 1900 as a recreational centre for the workers at Watt's Knutsford Steam Laundry, which you will encounter on your right at the bottom of Drury Lane. This, now converted into private residences, retains its original towers. The larger of the two formerly had a roof structure with a small spire, and was closely based on a tower which Watt had seen in Damascus. The laundry chimney, now demolished, was in the form of a minaret.

At the bottom of Drury Lane, follow the road right into Moorside Road. The buildings on your right are modern housing designed to blend with Watt's ideas. As you walk along, you will pass Coronation Building, built by Watt in 1902 to mark the coronation of Edward VII, and again showing Islamic influence.

A short distance now brings you back to the foot of King Street. If you would like to see more of what Watt did in Knutsford, the villas on Legh Road, which runs off the far end of Brook Street, will repay examination.

Places of Interest in the Neighbourhood
39. Offenders and Ordinands (Knutsford)
40. The Creator of Cranford (Knutsford)
41. The Home of Higgins the Highwayman (Knutsford)
42. Weightlifting for Would-be Wives (Lower Peover)
53. Where "Old Blood and Guts" had His Headquarters (Over Peover)

Gaskell memorial tower &
King's coffee house, Knutsford.   *The Ruskin Rooms, Knutsford.*

39 Offenders and Ordinands

Position: Knutsford
Ordnance Map: Stoke-on-Trent and Macclesfield area: Sheet 118:
1/50,000
Map Ref: SJ 752/784
Access: On the west side of Toft Road, approximately 100 yards north
of the railway station entrance.

Knutsford Sessions House, the solid Classical structure with an Ionic
portico, is the sole remaining portion of the House of Correction built
here in 1818 to the design of the famous Chester architect Thomas
Harrison. The huge gaol at the rear, capable of accommodating over
800 prisoners, was demolished in the 1930s.

It ceased to serve as a county gaol shortly before the First World War,
during which it housed prisoners of war and conscientious objectors.

After the war the building stood empty, and was taken over by Toc
H, the organisation founded in Flanders by the Reverend "Tubby"
Clayton, an army chaplain. Toc H (named after Talbot House, the
original soldiers' club set up by Clayton) used the gaol as an Ordination

Sessions House, Toft Road, Knutsford.

Test School, where former servicemen came to try their vocation to the ministry of the Church of England and, where needed, to acquire the necessary learning.

The students and teachers attended Knutsford Parish Church, and in the Memorial Chapel there is a brass lectern made from shell cases brought from the original Toc H chapel at Poperinghe. It was presented to the church by "Tubby" Clayton himself. Having fulfilled its intended purposes, the School closed in 1922. When the prison buildings were demolished, only the Sessions House was left, and there the Crown Court still sits.

Places of Interest in the Neighbourhood
38. Narrow Pavements – and Watt Architecture! (Knutsford)
40. The Creator of Cranford (Knutsford)
41. The Home of Higgins the Highwayman (Knutsford)

Mrs. Gaskell's grave, Brook Street Unitarian chapel graveyard, Knutsford.

40 The Creator of Cranford

Position: Knutsford
Ordnance Map: Stoke-on-Trent and Macclesfield area: Sheet 118:
1/50,000
Map Ref: SJ 754/783
Access: The Unitarian chapel is at the junction of Brook Street and
Adams Hill, on the south side.

Elizabeth Cleghorn Stephenson was born in Chelsea on 29th September 1810, and a year later her mother died. Her aunt, Mrs. Lumb,
adopted her and brought her back to her Knutsford home, "Heathwaite" in what is now Gaskell Avenue. Elizabeth lived there for four-
teen years before being sent to a boarding school in Stratford-on-Avon.
Her family were strong Unitarians, and by the time of her departure
from Knutsford she had become a Sunday-school teacher at Brook
Street Chapel (which is, incidentally, the oldest place of worship still in
use in Knutsford).

She married William Gaskell, minister of Cross Street Unitarian
Chapel, Manchester, on 30th August 1832 in Knutsford Parish Church.
(Unitarians were not permitted to marry in their own chapels until
1837). It was in Manchester that the couple made their home.

Mrs. Gaskell took up writing, with her husband's encouragement, as a
means of deadening the pain occasioned by the death of their only son
from scarlet fever. Her novels and short stories rapidly become popular
both in English-speaking countries, and elsewhere in translation. The
more serious novels, particularly, demonstrate the social concern that
so marked nineteenth-century Dissent.

She drew on her childhood memories for *Cranford*, the book for which
she is best remembered to-day. Many of the characters can be identified
with people she knew, and many of the locations can still be seen in
present-day Knutsford.

Cranford's creator died in Hampshire on 12th November 1865, and
her body was brought back to Knutsford for burial in the graveyard of
the chapel she had attended as a girl. Her grave is marked by a simple
cross, the one nearest to the end wall of the chapel.

Places of Interest in the Neighbourhood
38. Narrow Pavements – and Watt Architecture! (Kuntsford)
39. Offenders and Ordinands (Knutsford)
41. The Home of Higgins the Highwayman (Knutsford)

41 The Home of Higgins the Highwayman

Position: Knutsford
Ordnance Map: Stoke-on-Trent & Macclesfield area: Sheet 118:
1/50,000
Map Ref: SJ 748/786
Access: Heath House is situated in Gaskell Avenue, near its junction
with Stanley Road.

Numbers 19 and 20 Gaskell Avenue are now known as "Heath House",
but earlier the building was called "Heathfield", and before that "Cann
Office House". A Cann Office was a place where weights and measures
were tested. For about a decade in the mid-eighteenth century this
house, the name of which evokes ideas of fair dealing, was home to a
villain notorious both locally and further afield – Edward Higgins,
highwayman and housebreaker.

Not very much is known of Higgins before he came to Knutsford. He
was tried for sheep-stealing (then a capital offence) at Worcester in
1752, but was acquitted. Two years later, in the same place, he was
sentenced to seven years' transportation to the American colonies for
housebreaking. There he broke into a house in Boston and used the
proceeds to return to England. After a period in Manchester he settled
in Knutsford, where his marriage to Katherine Birtles on 21st April
1757 is recorded in the parish register. He gave his occupation then,
incidentally, as yeoman, and later, at the baptisms of his five children,
as gentleman.

For some years thereafter, Higgins "was on visiting terms, as well as
housebreaking terms, with the neighbouring gentry. He hunted with
them during the morning, dined with them in the afternoon, and made
himself familiar with their plate chests by night", in the words of a
nineteenth century Knutsford historian, Henry Green. As part of his
fictitious lifestyle as a country gentleman, he used to leave Knutsford
for a month or two every year on the pretext of going to collect his
rents. He invariably returned well supplied with cash, and crimes as far
away as Gloucester, Bristol and Carmarthenshire are said to have been
carried out by him during these absences.

It was at Carmarthen, in 1767, that Higgins's luck ran out. He was
tried there for housebreaking, convicted and executed on 7th November, after a last-minute attempt to cheat the hangman by having an
accomplice send a forged reprieve. He left behind, besides his wife and

children (who knew nothing of his criminal activities), a detailed confession of his crimes, which included murder. A short story based on him, *The Squire's Tale*, was written by Mrs. Gaskell, whose early years were spent close by at "Heathwaite", 17 Gaskell Avenue.

Places of Interest in the Neighbourhood
38. Narrow Pavements – and Watt Architecture (Knutsford)
39. Offenders and Ordinands (Knutsford)
40. The Creator of Cranford (Knutsford)
42. Weightlifting for Would-be Wives (Lower Peover)
53. Where "Old Blood and Guts" had His Headquarters (Over Peover)

Heathfield, Gaskell Avenue, Knutsford.

42 Weightlifting for Would-be Wives

Position: Lower Peover, between Middlewich and Knutsford
Ordnance Map: Stoke-on-Trent & Macclesfield area: Sheet 118:
1/50,000
Map Ref: SJ 743/741
Access: The church of St. Oswald lies to the east of the B.5081 road. It
is open daily.

There was a chapel on this site as early as 1269, and the present building
probably dates from about a century later, with the tower being added
in 1582.

One of the church's treasures is a huge chest, hollowed out from a
single piece of oak. In the days before farm mechanisation, when all
dairy work had to be done by hand, the tasks involved in the making of
butter or cheese required a pair of strong arms. It was reckoned locally
that only a young woman who could lift the chest's massive lid one-
handed was strong enough to be a Cheshire dairy farmer's wife.

What the young farmers of the day thought of the prospect of
marriage to the possessor of such muscle-power is not recorded.

Places of Interest in the Neighbourhood
38. Narrow Pavements – and Watt Architecture! (Knutsford)
39. Offenders and Ordinands (Knutsford)
40. The Creator of Cranford (Knutsford)
41. The Home of Higgins the Highwayman (Knutsford)
53. Where "Old Blood and Guts" had His Headquarters (Over Peover)

The Bow Stones, Lyme Handley.

72

43 The Bow Stones

Position: Lyme Handley, near Disley
Ordnance Map: Manchester and surrounding area: Sheet 109: 1/50,000
Map Ref: SJ 974/813
Access: The stones stand on the west side of the unclassified road in a small enclosure to which a stile gives access.

Over a century ago, at a time when antiquaries held the Druids responsible for practically all ancient remains, they were considered Druidical – ordinary locals, however, thought they had some connection with Robin Hood.

The two stones must have acquired their name in fairly recent times, for they are in fact the upper parts of the shafts of double Anglo-Saxon crosses of a type found in north-east Cheshire and adjoining areas of Derbyshire, dating from the 9th or 10th centuries, and the spot where they now stand is certainly not where they were originally erected.

The most attractive, and plausible, theory ties them to two cross-heads, now at Lyme Park, which were ploughed up in a field near Disley Church about 1845, and to a double-socketed cross-base dug up in the Church Field, Disley, in 1956. Both the cross-heads and the base match the Bow Stones in terms of style and decoration (and therefore date) and dimensions.

Following the Reformation there was a wave of destruction of crosses throughout the country. Evidence suggests that the two crosses in Disley churchyard were broken up around 1548, and that some time after that the larger parts of the shafts were set up at Bow Stone Gate, probably by Sir Piers Legh of Lyme, who died in 1590. They stand at the intersection of two long-established routes, and he may have intended them as boundary markers, guide posts, wayside shrines (they have crosses cut into them, and Sir Piers was accused of favouring the old ideas in religion), or all three.

Scattered on the moors nearby are a number of inscribed stones which mark the graves of victims of an outbreak of plague in 1646. Their bodies must have been interred as quickly as possible in the hope of avoiding infection.

Places of Interest in the Neighbourhood
13. Symbol of Bollington's Industrial Past (Bollington)
57. Culture for the Colliers (Poynton)
58. To Quench the Thirst of Man and Beast (Poynton)

44 "Careless, Intemperate and Improvident"

Position: Lymm
Ordnance Map: Manchester and surrounding area: Sheet 109: 1/50,000
Map Ref: SJ 691/866
Access: In Arley Grove, which runs off Higher Lane.

Unexpectedly, in that Arley Grove consists almost entirely of modern developments, one comes across numbers 1 to 7, a row of three-storey cottages. They date from the early nineteenth century, and the third storey would originally have been a continuous space stretching the full length of the terrace. The reason is that the principal industry in Lymm, then and for some time thereafter, was fustian-cutting, which necessitated large workrooms, or "lofts" as they were called.

Fustian was a cotton twill fabric woven with a looped finish on the weft threads. By running a special knife along these loops, the cutter produced a cloth with a pile, the finest weave being called velvet and a coarser variety velveteen.

A "piece" of fustian 100 yards long and 20 or 30 inches wide would arrive from Manchester for cutting. In the loft it would be stretched tightly over a frame in "lengths" of six feet at a time. The cutter, leaning to the right over the length, inserted the tip of the knife into the furthest "race" or row of loops and walked the six-foot length, thus making the first cut of the pile. After walking back, the process would be repeated on the next nearest race. A fine velvet would have 800 to 900 races in its 20 inch width, and at 50 lengths to a piece this would mean over 40,000 cuts to be made before the piece was finished.

Children very often began work in the trade at nine years old. The continual leaning to the right over the frame meant that, in the words of a local doctor giving evidence to a Royal Commission on the Employment of Children in 1862 " . . . the defect of figure is very conspicuous and prevalent; the distortion inwards of the right knee is most so . . . " and "The high shoulder, which is another deformity among cutters, if it were of an aggravated form, would be accompanied by distortion of the spine."

The fine particles from the cut pile, or the deliberately damp atmosphere designed to lay the dust, made the trade even more unhealthy.

Because the cutting operation was so difficult to mechanise, cutters could earn high wages when times were good, but the fact that they were paid by the piece, plus the ups and downs of the cotton trade, did not encourage sober habits. To quote another witness before the Royal Commission:

"I am the relieving officer here in Lymm. The cutters are a bad lot; careless, intemperate and improvident."

Around 1920 fustian-cutting machinery was developed and cutting by hand died a very speedy death. Now no complete original example of a fustian-cutting knife is known to exist in Lymm, the only reminder of the slavery which King Cotton imposed, not on a Lancashire mill town, but on a rural Cheshire village, being these and other premises where the trade was carried on.

Places of Interest in the Neighbourhood

Terrace of Fustian-cutters' cottages, Lymm.

45 Six Centuries of Worship

Position: Marton, north of Congleton
Ordnance Map: Stoke-on-Trent and Macclesfield area: Sheet 118:
1/50,000
Map Ref: SJ 850/680
Access: On the east side of the A.34 road from Alderley Edge to
Congleton.

The Church of St. James and St. Paul was founded by Sir John de
Davenport about the middle of the fourteenth century. The chancel and
side chapels were found to be suffering from decay in the eighteenth
century and were rebuilt in brick instead of the original timber. The
roof was lowered in 1804 and further restoration work was carried
out in 1850 and again in 1871. In spite of these vicissitudes the building remains extremely attractive internally and externally, and proudly
claims to be the oldest timber-framed church in Europe still in use.

Places of Interest in the Neighbourhood
29. "Old Maggoty" or "Lord Flame"? (Gawsworth)
30. Where the Dark Lady Walks (Gawsworth)
35. The Village that Fell Asleep (Havannah)

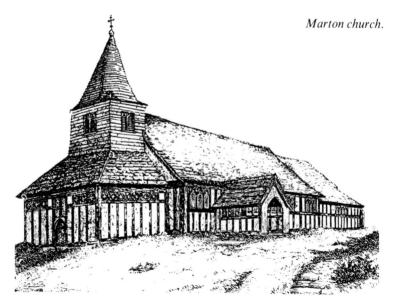

Marton church.

46 Squire Wilbraham's Early Folly and a Religious Revival

Position: Mow Cop, between Congleton and Kidsgrove
Ordnance Map: Stoke-on-Trent and Macclesfield area: Sheet 118: 1/50,000
Map Ref: SJ 888/574
Access: From the car park at the north end of High Street.

A landmark over a wide area, Mow Cop Castle was never a castle at all. Its importance lies in the fact that it was one of the earliest examples of a folly in the country. Randle Wilbraham of Rode Hall, some 2½ miles to the west, had it built in 1754 to improve the view from his family seat. In doing so he may have been following the latest architectural fashion while relieving local unemployment. The mason work was carried out by a local family named Harding, one of whom lost two fingers in an accident during the building.

The ridge on which the tower stands is the boundary between two counties (Cheshire and Staffordshire), two dioceses (Chester and Lichfield) and two archiepiscopal provinces (Canterbury and York). It was

Mow Cop Castle.

presumably this border status that led to its becoming a place of resort for local Roman Catholics in penal times. In 1642 they were stated to be meeting on Mow Cop for mass "and other common prayers in Latin".

Mow Cop's main religious significance, however, is as the birthplace of Primitive Methodism. Hugh Bourne, a local Methodist preacher who was fired by the Camp Meeting movement then sweeping America, organised the first such meeting in England at the summit of Mow Cop on Sunday 31st May 1807. This was soon followed by more ambitious and better organised events both here and elsewhere.

Camp Meetings met with disapproval from the English Methodist establishment, and within a few years the Primitive Methodists (referred to as 'Ranters' by some) had emerged as a separate denomination, remaining so until the Methodist Reunion of 1932.

Five years after that event, a unique Camp Meeting was held here, in the course of which the deeds of the folly and six acres of surrounding land were given to the National Trust by Mr. Joseph Lovatt, a local man and lifelong Wesleyan Methodist who had bought the land some fifteen years earlier.

The importance of the site in the history of Methodism is to-day commemorated by an inscribed stone beside the path from the car park to the folly tower.

Places of Interest in the Neighbourhood

Lieutenant Brown's memorial, Nantwich.

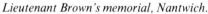

47 A Sacrifice Still Remembered

Position: Nantwich
Ordnance Map: Stoke-on-Trent & Macclesfield area: Sheet 118:
1/50,000
Map Ref: SJ 648/516
Access: Go south along Shrewbridge Road. Cross over the level
crossing, and after the last house on the right, turn right on to a small
parking area. From here a riverside path runs to the right, behind the
houses just passed. Follow this and after a few yards the memorial will
come into sight on the right.

On 14th January 1944 Lieutenant Arthur L. Brown, United States
Army Air Force, was flying over Cheshire at the controls of a P-47
Thunderbolt fighter-bomber. The purpose of his flight was to test new
oxygen equipment. Over Nantwich, his engine suddenly failed.

Eyewitnesses on the ground reported that the pilot deliberately
steered the doomed aircraft away from the densely populated town
centre, and it finally nose-dived into an area of quicksand near the
River Weaver. Neither the aircraft nor Lieutenant Brown's body was
ever recovered. He was aged 23 at the time of his death.

His self-sacrificing action ensured that he was remembered locally,
though. The owner of the field leading down to the river at the crash
site, a local ironmonger, put up a memorial in the form of a dummy
grave. A local Brownie pack made regular visits with flowers, and one
of their leaders kept up the practice until 1985, when the local branch of
the Cheshire Regiment Association took over the care of the memorial.

By that time, it was in poor condition, and a local stonemason offered
to provide a new stone free of charge. Other local people helped with
the restoration in various ways, and the new memorial was eventually
dedicated in the course of a service conducted by a local clergyman who
was a wartime R.A.F. fighter pilot and attended by Lieutenant Brown's
sister from New York. Wreaths are laid in tribute on the memorial each
Remembrance Sunday.

Places of Interest in the Neighbourhood
1. The End of the Game? (Acton)
48. From the Ashes of a Vehement Fire (Nantwich)
69. Stoke Hall Dovecote (Stoke)

79

48 From the Ashes of a Vehement Fire

Position: Nantwich
Ordnance Map: Stoke-on-Trent and Macclesfield area: Sheet 118:
1/50,000
Map Ref: SJ 652/522
Access: On the east side of High Street.

The 'Supercigs' frontage at street level is hardly calculated to make
the viewer pause, but as the eye travels upwards it becomes clear that
this is one of the buildings which formed part of the reconstruction of
Nantwich after the Great Fire of December 1583.

In the words of an eyewitness account:

> "The X Day of this Month chaunced a most tereble and vehement fyre
> begining at the waterlode about vi of the clocke at night, in a kitchen by
> Bruinge, the winde being very boysterous increased ye sayd fyre, which
> very vehemently wasted and consumed (in the space of 15 hours) 600
> bays of buildings"

The efforts of the firefighters, ineffectual at the best of times in those
days, were further hampered by the fact that four bears had been let out
of their stables at the back of the Bear Inn by their owner and the
landlord. The women who were carrying buckets of water were terrified
and would only work after being provided with an armed guard. By the
time the fire burnt itself out next day 132 properties had been destroyed
and three women killed, a providentially small loss of life.

A national appeal fund was launched, the list of names being headed
by that of Queen Elizabeth, who subscribed £1,000.

High Street was the richest area of the town at the time of the fire, and
it is here that the finest examples of post-fire rebuilding can be seen.
These may also have been among the first properties reconstructed. The
Queen's Aid House was certainly built within a year of the disaster, as
the inscriptions on its "magpie" frontage reveal:

> God Grante Our Ryal Queen
> In England Longe to Raign
> For She Hath Put Her Helping
> Hand to Bild This Towne Again.

And underneath:

> Thomas Cleese Made This Worke The Yeare
> of our Lorde God 1584.

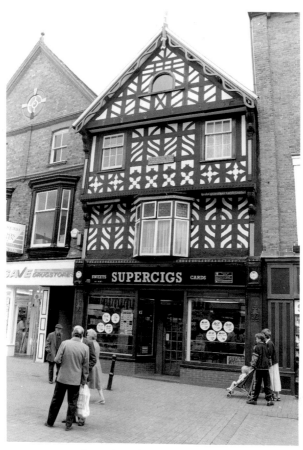

Queen's Aid House, Nantwich.

Seven years earlier carpenter Cleese had built Churche's Mansion in Hospital Street, which, being on the outskirts of the town, had survived the fire. He also built the roofs of the north and south transepts of the parish church. He and other craftsmen in the construction industry must have enjoyed something of a boom, and many buildings which rose from the ashes of the Great Fire stand to this day, adding greatly to the charm of old Nantwich.

Places of Interest in the Neighbourhood

49 An Elizabethan Corn Mill

Position: Nether Alderley
Ordnance Map: Stoke-on-Trent and Macclesfield area: Sheet 118:
1/500,000
Map Ref: SJ 843/762
Access: On the east side of the A.34 road. The mill is a National Trust
property: check opening times and admission charges.

This is the oldest of Cheshire's restored water-powered corn mills (the
others are at Stretton, near Malpas, and Bunbury). The present building probably dates from the sixteenth century, though there is evidence
of a Saxon mill on this site.

   Its most striking exterior feature is the very long sloping flagged roof,
which almost reaches down to the ground at the front. Another notable
characteristic is that this mill has two driving wheels, one above the
other. Both are of the overshot type and measure twelve feet diameter
with a width of three feet.

   The mill worked until 1939, and the restored machinery, originally
installed around 1850, is occasionally used to grind flour for
demonstration.

Places of Interest in the Neighbourhood
  2. The Wizard and Mr. Garner (Alderley Edge)
 32. Contrasting Faces of a Baptist Chapel (Great Warford)
 78. Romany's Garden of Remembrance (Wilmslow)

Nether Alderley Mill.

50 It Floats! It Swings!! It's Electric!!!

Position: Northwich
Ordnance Map: Stoke-on-Trent and Macclesfield area: Sheet 118:
1/50,000
Map Ref: SJ 565/738
Access: Town Bridge is the main entry into Northwich from the west.

The Town Bridge was built in its present form in 1899 to the designs of
J.E. Saner, chief engineer to the Weaver Navigation Trustees. Bridges
over the Weaver had to be moveable to allow vessels to proceed
upstream as far as Winsford. Northwich had the additional problems of
subsidence due to salt workings, which meant that a building (or a
bridge) was liable to disappear, suddenly or gradually, into the earth.

Saner solved the problem by arranging for some three-fifths of the
weight of the bridge to be borne by a floating pontoon, which turns with
the bridge structure. The remainder is carried by eight linked steel piles
round the outside of the pontoon which carry a roller path on which the
bridge swings. The height of the roller path can be adjusted to counter-
act subsidence and keep the bridge swinging true.

The swinging mechanism was driven by electricity from the beginning,
which makes Town Bridge and the contemporary and similar Hayhurst
Bridge upstream the oldest electric swing bridges in the world.

Places of Interest in the Neighbourhood
  6. Unique in this Country – First in the World (Anderton)
65. A Famous Foxhound (Sandiway)
79. Giants of the Chemical Industry (Winnington)

Town Bridge, Northwich.

51 The Old Woman of Delamere Forest

Position: Oakmere, near Tarporley
Ordnance Map: Chester, Wrexham & surrounding area: Sheet 117: 1/50,000
Map Ref: SJ 575/677
Access: No public access, but views of the Mere can be obtained from the A.54 road, west of its intersection with the A.49.

Hard on the heels of news of the victory at Waterloo, further excitement came to the Delamere Forest area in the summer of 1815. A local sensation was created by the sudden appearance of a woman and her daughter, with all their possessions in a donkey cart, plus two goats.

The woman's name was Anna Maria Hollingsworth (which is how she usually signed herself – local people sometimes anglicised her to Mary Anne). She had been born at Leeuwarden in West Friesland fifty years earlier, the daughter of a Lutheran clergyman. Later she had married an English soldier, and had followed him until he was killed at the siege of Bergen op Zoom in 1814.

She had then brought her son and daughter to England, where some Hanoverian friends had arranged an apprenticeship for the son in Hanover. Setting out to look for a permanent home, she and her daughter had been continually moved on by parish officials who were anxious not to have them as a burden on the rates. Stopping at Oakmere for a day or two to wash her clothes, she heard (wrongly in fact), that the area, the property of Lord Delamere, was extra-parochial, and so on 17th July she wrote in broken English to Lady Delamere at Vale Royal, asking leave to settle down for a few weeks.

Permission granted, she built a rough shelter of turves and branches on a rising bank near the mere. It had as its basis two ribs of a whale which had been erected there years before by Philip Egerton of nearby Oulton. As time passed, she and her daughter were able to improve it, to enclose half an acre as a garden, and to keep hens, the daughter taking eggs and garden produce to sell at Tarporley market.

The "few weeks" extended into years, and Mrs. Hollingworth taught reading and writing to local children until about 1820, when various quarrels with neighbours arose. Eventually she sent her daughter to her Hanoverian contacts in London to be found a situation, which was done, and later, as her age and infirmities increased, her London friends secured her admission to one of the Dutch almshouses in the capital.

The Old Woman of Delamere Forest, Oakmere.

There she was living in 1832 when an account of her Cheshire sojourn was written.

Before she left Oakmere, she brought to Lady Delamere at Vale Royal two gifts, one a German prayer book, and the other the last descendant of the goats she had brought with her in 1815, together with a dedicatory verse.

Places of Interest in the Neighbourhood
52. Imprisoned Below Stairs? (Over)
66. Guardian of the Dual Carriageway (Sandiway)
76. Birthplace of the Cheshire Prophet (Whitegate)

52 Imprisoned Below Stairs?

Position: Over, near Winsford
Ordnance Map: Stoke-on-Trent and Macclesfield area: Sheet 118:
1/50,000
Map Ref: SJ 638/661
Access: On the east side of Delamere Street, immediately south of St.
John's School.

Over Cross, although a large enough structure, is now rather incon-
spicuous owing to the trees around it having grown and consequently
tending to overshadow it.

It was erected in the 1840s as a market cross. This was part of a bid to
re-establish a market in this part of the town and to regain trade which
had been lost to a market situated near the River Weaver. The adjacent
part of the school next door, incidentally, was built as a market hall at
the same time, and only adapted for use as a school after the attempt to
revive Over Market failed.

The cross, apparently, originally stood further forward on the pavement, since in 1887-88 £1. 7s. 6d. was spent on moving it back a few
feet. As built, it was surrounded with iron railings, but these went for
munitions in the Second World War and were never replaced.

The most curious feature of the structure can be viewed by going
round to the back of it. There, the lower steps are replaced by a flat
wall with a doorway. Tradition declares that the space inside was used
as a lock-up. If so, confinement in it must have been harsh, even by
Victorian standards. Certainly its recorded use in later years was much
more prosaic – as a coal store.

Places of Interest in the Neighbourhood
51. The Old Woman of Delamere Forest (Oakmere)
65. A Famous Foxhound (Sandiway)
66. Guardian of the Dual Carriageway (Sandiway)
76. Birthplace of the Cheshire Prophet (Whitegate)

53 Where "Old Blood and Guts" had His Headquarters

Position: Over Peover, south of Knutsford
Ordnance Map: Stoke-on-Trent & Macclesfield area: Sheet 118: 1/50,000
Map Ref: SJ 767/746
Access: At junction of A.50 Knutsford – Holmes Chapel road and unclassified road by the Whipping Stocks pub.

This early nineteenth-century lodge is an attractive building in its own right, its most unusual feature being the knotted tree trunks which form the angles of the walls. The gate by which it stands is the entrance to the drive to Peover Hall. In the period leading up to the invasion of Europe in 1944, two or three hundred American soldiers lived in huts in the park, for the Hall had been requisitioned as the headquarters of General George S. Patton, United States Army.

It would have been through this gateway that Patton would have been driven to Knutsford on 25th January, 1944. He went to attend the formal opening of a club for American servicemen called the "Donut Dugout", operated by the local Women's Voluntary Service.

Lodge to Peover Hall, Over Peover.

In the course of his speech, Patton expressed his personal view that, after the war, the world would be ruled by America, Britain and Russia. Unfortunately, in the version reported in the United States, the reference to Russia was omitted, and he was at once condemned for slighting so important an ally.

The aggressive style of leadership which made "Gorgeous Georgie" probably the best handler of armour among the western Allies had already got him into trouble on more than one occasion, and this incident led to his not receiving a major command during the Normandy landings. Instead, his Third Army, which remained in England on D-Day, was able to make a very rapid major advance across Europe once the beachhead had been consolidated.

Peover Hall itself, a mile to the south-east, is occasionally open to the public. The Georgian part in which Patton resided has been demolished, but the room used as the Officers' Mess survives in the earlier part of the building.

Places of Interest in the Neighbourhood
38. Narrow Pavements – and Watt Architecture! (Knutsford)
39. Offenders and Ordinands (Knutsford)
40. The Creator of Cranford (Knutsford)
41. The Home of Higgins the Highwayman (Knutsford)
42. Weightlifting for Would-be Wives (Lower Peover)

Cottages, Parkgate.

54 Lady Hamilton and Nelson

Position: Parkgate, near Neston
Ordnance Map: Chester, Wrexham and surrounding area: Sheet 117:
1/50,000
Map Ref: SJ 280/779
Access: From Neston town centre, follow signs for Parkgate. The two
cottages are at the bottom of the hill as you turn sharp right on to the
Parade. The best approach is to park on the Parade, patronise one of
Parkgate's home-made ice cream shops, and enjoy your treat as you
walk back round the corner.

Incredible as it seems now, Parkgate in the 18th century, before the rise
of Liverpool, was the North West's premier port for trade with Ireland.
Handel and John Wesley are but two of the well-known names who
passed through here before the river silted up and the marsh-grass took
over.

Of the two cottages at the bottom of Station road, the one nearest the
river (Number 16) is reputed to be the house where the then Emma
Lyon (born not far away at Ness) stayed in June 1784 when she came
here to bathe in the sea water to try to cure a skin complaint. This was
before she became Lady Hamilton and the mistress of Lord Nelson.

The area in front of the adjoining cottage (Number 15) is made up of
light-coloured pebbles, among which the word NELSON is picked out
in black pebbles. This has led in the past to various speculations and
flights of fancy, but the true explanation is as follows.

In the early 19th century the cottage was used as a summer retreat by
Albin Burt, a Chester artist who specialised in miniature portraits. Presumably he was an admirer of the great admiral, for he called his son
Nelson and his daughter Emma. In December 1822, Burt and his son
were crossing the River Mersey from Liverpool to Ellesmere Port on
board the paddle steamer *Prince Regent*. A severe storm arose and
Nelson Burt was swept overboard and drowned.

His grieving father used to gather the stones along the shore of the
Dee, and set Nelson's name in black pebbles outside his cottage as a
memorial. About sixty years ago they were set in cement to preserve
them.

Places of Interest in the Neighbourhood
18. One Hand on the Clock – Two Graves in the Wood (Burton)
68. Cheshire's Gretna Green (Shotwick)

55 The Elephant and Castle

Position: Peckforton
Ordnance Map: Chester, Wrexham and surrounding area: Sheet 117:
1/50,000
Map Ref: SJ 537/565
Access: On the west side of Stone House Lane, just north of the
junction with Peckforton Hall Lane. The elephant is best viewed from
the road which runs just north of Laundry Cottage.

This amusing and striking piece of whimsy is an example of the leisure
activity of a Victorian craftsman. It was carved around 1859 by a local
stonemason named Watson (his Christian name is variously given as
William or John) who was working at that time on Peckforton Castle.
He had earlier been foreman mason during the construction of the
Grosvenor Bridge at Chester, and is known to have carved two pairs of
stone lions which now adorn houses at Spurstow and Tattenhall.

Why Mr. Watson chose the elephant and castle as a subject is not
known. Such a creature features in the arms of the Corbett family, who
owned Peckforton up to about 1626, and this may have been his
inspiration. He used stone from the same quarry as that used for
Peckforton Castle, and originally set the carving up in the garden of his
own cottage. When that cottage was demolished, the elephant was
moved to its present site.

A curious feature is that some of the windows of the castle contain
glass. It is said that Watson originally made it with all its windows
glazed, and that it was intended to be used as a beehive. There is,
however, no indication that this was ever done.

Places of Interest in the Neighbourhood
12. The Best of British Castramentation (Bickerton)
17. The Poacher's Revenge (Bunbury)
28. The Copper Mine Chimney (Gallantry Bank)

(For illustration see Frontispiece)

56 From Hermit to Archbishop

Position: Plemstall, 3 ½ miles north-east of Chester
Ordnance Map: Chester, Wrexham and surrounding area: Sheet 117:
1/50,000
Map Ref: SJ 457/701
Access: Along Plemstall Lane (signposted "Plemstall Church"), which
runs east off the A.56 road, just north of the crossroads at Mickle
Trafford.

A thousand years ago the area around Plemstall was undrained
marshland, frequently flooded, and the church, dedicated to St. Peter, is
said, probably fancifully, to owe its original foundation to a fisherman
who was washed ashore there and built it in thanksgiving for his
survival.

    To this inhospitable spot, in the second half of the ninth century, came
a Mercian cleric named Plegmund, to live as a hermit. In spite of his
isolated habitation, his learning and holy life became widely known,
and when Alfred the Great came to the throne of England he summoned Plegmund to his court, where he tutored the King and helped
him with his literary work. Plegmund is said (doubtfully) to have com-
plied and written the first part of the Winchester Codex of the *Anglo-
Saxon Chronicle*, but it is certain that he helped Alfred with his version

Church of St Peter, Plemstall.

of Pope Gregory's *Regula Pastoralis*, for his assistance is acknowledged in the preface.

He became Archbishop of Canterbury in 890, and thus it fell to him to crown Alfred's son Edward in 901. As Archbishop, he twice undertook the then lengthy journey to Rome, on his second visit, in 908, carrying to Pope Sergius III the alms sent by King Ethelweard. He died at an advanced age in 914, and was buried in his cathedral at Canterbury.

On the north side of Plemstall Lane, just to the west of the little bridge, can be seen the site of the spring known as St. Plegmund's Well. A long-standing and credible tradition says that here was where the saint used to baptise his converts. Although restored early this century, it was dry when I last visited it, and its surrounding slabs were fenced off with orange plastic mesh.

If the church is open, it is well worth viewing the superb woodcarving inside. The roofing is medieval, and some other work is of early date, but most of it was carved in the first half of this century by the Rev. Joseph Toogood, who was incumbent here from 1907 to 1946. Truly a case of "If you seek a monument . . . "

Places of Interest in the Neighbourhood
  5. Moving House – Literally (Alvanley)
 10. The Last Great Cockfight (Ashton)
 20. A Zoo in the Basement (Christleton)
 36. Where Packhorses Plodded (Hockenhull Platts)

Cottages (formerly library & newsroom) Poynton.

57 Culture for the Colliers

Position: Poynton
Ordnance Map: Manchester & surrounding area: Sheet 109: 1/50,000
Map Ref: SJ 921/838
Access: On east side of London Road North (nos. 44 and 46).

These two delightfully ornate Victorian cottages were originally a single building, designed as a library and newsroom. In the nineteenth century Poynton was a coalmining village, and the story really begins in 1854 when John Hadwen, a colliery manager, gave £500 to set up an institution aimed at improving the moral and intellectual standards of the mining community. The building itself was provided by the colliery owner, Lord Vernon, and by 1855 the library had 500 volumes and subscribed to a number of magazines. It was described and depicted in the *Illustrated London News* of June 1854 as a model for other mine owners to follow.

By 1880 the level of provision had more than quadrupled, and the local newspaper proudly proclaimed that "In no village of the same size and importance in the county can be found a nicer little reading room and library than the one at Poynton".

The good work continued until after the First World War, when new legislation gave county councils the ability to provide library services. The building was retained by the Vernon Estate and converted into cottages, with a second storey being added (which accounts for the dormer windows). The porch was also slightly altered to accommodate two doors instead of one.

Places of Interest in the Neighbourhood
13. Symbol of Bollington's Industrial Past (Bollington)
14. White Nancy (Bollington)
43. The Bow Stones (Lyme Handley)
58. To Quench the Thirst of Man and Beast (Poynton)

58 To Quench the Thirst of Man and Beast

Position: Poynton
Ordnance Map: Manchester and surrounding area: Sheet 109: 1/50,000
Map Ref: SJ 919/836
Access: On traffic island at road junction by Poynton Church.

When the inhabitants of Poynton decided to commemorate Queen
Victoria's Diamond Jubilee in 1897, they seem to have done so with an
eye to obtaining value for money. They paid £212 for this delightfully
ornate piece of work in cast iron, and for that sum they acquired an
item of street furniture which combined the roles of lamp standard,
guide post and drinking fountain.

The four directional plates survive, as do the four lamps (which were
originally lit by gas). The fountain is no longer operational, its water
receptacles now being filled with flowering plants.

But the good Poyntonians were not thinking only of their own welfare
when they ordered their fountain from Wilson & Co. of Manchester.
The lion masks on three sides of the plinth would have produced, in
their heyday, a jet of water, which fell into a square basin (for humans),
thence into a semi-circular basin (for horses) and finally into a bowl (for
dogs).

Places of Interest in the Neighbourhood
13. Symbol of Bollington's Industrial Past (Bollington)
43. The Bow Stones (Lyme Handley)
57. Culture for the Colliers (Poynton)

59 An early Exercise in Conservation

Position: Prestbury
Ordnance Map: Stoke-on-Trent & Macclesfield area: Sheet 118:
1/50,000
Map Ref: SJ 901/768
Access: In village centre, behind the church (follow signposts in churchyard).

One major difference between the counties of the north and west of England and those of the south and east is the much greater number of multiple-township parishes in the former. Prestbury parish at one time included no fewer than thirty-five townships, and the church here was the most important in east Cheshire.

There is a long history of worship on this site. The present church of St. Peter dates originally from 1220, with many later additions, alterations and restorations, but in a glass case in the churchyard can be seen an 8th century preaching cross. This was reconstructed from fragments found embedded in the chancel wall in 1841.

Nearby stands the present church's predecessor – a Norman chapel probably built on the site of an earlier Saxon structure towards the end of the 12th century. An inscription above the doorway on the west side records that it was restored in 1747 by Sir William Meredith of Macclesfield.

How much is original and how much 18th century is not easy to decide. The arched doorway with the row of carved figures above is certainly Norman, while the glass in the windows certainly is not – they were only dedicated in 1977.

Sir William's shade deserves thanks for his pioneer effort, and must look down contented that his work is still preserved in its turn.

Places of Interest in the Neighbourhood
13. Symbol of Bollington's Industrial Past (Bollington)
14. White Nancy (Bollington)
60. Once a Vicarage – Now a Bank (Prestbury)
61. The Mystery of the Woman's Footprint (Rainow)

60 Once a Vicarage – Now a Bank

Position: Prestbury
Ordnance Map: Stoke-on-Trent and Macclesfield area: Sheet 118:
1/50,000
Map Ref: SJ 900/769
Access: On main village street, opposite the church.

The Prestbury branch of the National Westminster Bank began its life
with a very different purpose. Generally known as the Priest's House, it
was formerly the local vicarage.

The building, delightfully lopsided, has its origins in the sixteenth
century, but much of the surviving work dates from the 1600s. It was
this period which saw what were probably the building's most exciting
days; there is an old tradition that the incumbent preached from the
balcony over the doorway when he was barred from the church under
the Commonwealth.

A new vicarage was built in 1708, and the Priest's House was divided
into cottages, remaining so for over 200 years, until just before the First
World War when it was condemned as unfit for use as a dwelling-house.
It was subsequently opened as an antique shop.

The building was completely and sympathetically restored in 1968-70.
Although the interior has been much altered to meet banking require-
ments, two cast-iron firebacks found during the restoration can be seen
in the banking hall. The older is dated 1635 and bears the arms of King
Charles I.

Places of Interest in the Neighbourhood
13. Symbol of Bollington's Industrial Past (Bollington)
14. White Nancy (Bollington)
59. An early Exercise in Conservation (Prestbury)

The Old Vicarage, Prestbury.

61 The Mystery of the Woman's Footprint

Position: Rainow
Ordnance Map: Stoke-on-Trent & Macclesfield area: Sheet 118:
Map Ref: SJ 977/759
Access: On the east side of Ewrin Lane, between Buxter Stoops farm and the junction with Hooleyhey Lane.

John Turner's memorial stone commemorates a truly mysterious occurrence. The 29-year old son of Richard Turner of nearby Saltersford Hall, John ran a team of packhorses in the area. On Christmas Eve 1735 he was returning home from one of his trips. When he reached Bollington a snowstorm was raging and he was urged to stay there overnight. However, he insisted on pressing on towards the family home. That was the last time he was seen alive . . . or was it?

The stone is inscribed on both sides. The southern one reads:

> HERE JOHN TUR
> NER WAS CAST
> AWAY IN A HEAVY
> SNOWSTORM IN
> THE NIGHT IN OR
> ABOUT THE YEAR
> 1755

The discrepancy in date is accounted for by the fact that the stone now visible is said to be the third one marking the spot. The original was erected by James Mellor of Hough Hole House, and the inscription must have been incorrectly copied when a replacement was carved.

The mystery is recorded on the northern side of the stone:

> THE PRINT OF A
> WOMANS SHOE WAS
> FOUND BY HIS SIDE
> IN THE SNOW WERE
> HE LAY DEAD
> H

No explanation has ever been found.

Places of Interest in the Neighbourhood
13. Symbol of Bollington's Industrial Past (Bollington)
14. White Nancy (Bollington)
33. Where the Schemer Learned His Trade (Gurnett)

62 Paratroops Smelt Mermaid

Position: Rostherne, north of Knutsford
Ordnance Map: Manchester and surrounding area: Sheet 109: 1/50,000
Map Ref: SJ 742/838
Access: There is no public access to Rostherne Mere, which is a
National Nature Reserve. A good view of the Mere can be obtained
from the churchyard.

Transport yourself back, if you will, fifty years as you stand or sit by
Rostherne Church, overlooking the Mere, the largest sheet of inland
water in Cheshire.

Away to the east, the pre-war Manchester Airport has been taken over
by the Royal Air Force as No. 1 Parachute Training School, Ringway.
Just to the south, the Egerton family's Tatton Park estate serves as a
dropping zone for trainee paratroopers.

A faint sound of aero-engines grows louder, and into view, in its
characteristic nose-down attitude, comes a Whitley bomber. These
aircraft give the airborne soldiers their introduction to parachuting
from an aeroplane through a hole in the floor. From the Whitley drops
one man – then another – then another, until the sky over the Mere is
dotted with parachutes, each with a tiny figure dangling below it. Each
one drops into the Mere, releases his parachute, and is picked up by
boat.

Such "water jumps" were a regular Christmas pastime for instructors
at Ringway and, with more serious intent, formed part of the training of
the men and women agents of Special Operations Executive, whose
tasks involved being parachuted into occupied Europe under cover of
darkness.

The smelt, otherwise known as the sparling, is a species of salt-water
fish which used frequently to be caught in Rostherne Mere. How it
came to live and breed in the Mere's fresh water has never been explained, and no specimen of the fish has been recorded here since the
local naturalist T.A. Coward saw one on 31st March 1922. This is in
spite of a systematic programme of netting in the Mere between 1962
and 1965.

Oddly enough, the first mention of smelt in the Mere, published in
1686, says that they were netted only at Eastertide. Another reputed
visitor to the Mere at that season was a mermaid who was supposed to
appear on the surface at daybreak every Easter Sunday. Her arrival was
said to be via an underwater tunnel leading from the River Mersey.

Could the original stock of smelt have followed her?

Places of Interest in the Neighbourhood

Water Tower, Saighton.

63 Guardian of the Pass

Position: Saighton, south-east of Chester
Ordnance Map: Chester, Wrexham & surrounding area: Sheet 117:
1/50,000
Map Ref: SJ 443/619
Access: On east side of Chapel Lane, 100 yards north of Abbey Gate
School.

Approaching Saighton from the south, the skyline seems to be
dominated by a squat castellated tower built in red sandstone. Closer
still, the road enters a rock cutting and the tower's loopholes become
visible. One has a strong impression of a fortified tower looming over a
defile to block the passage of invaders.

Then, as one rounds the corner and reaches the base of the tower, the
scale seems to change. It no longer appears so massive, and the smooth
blocks of which it is composed suggest a recent rather than a medieval
origin.

In fact, the tower's purpose was never warlike – it is simply a water
tower, dating from about 1870.

Places of Interest in the Neighbourhood
  3. An Original "Telford" (Aldford)
  4. The Duke's Dispensary (Aldford)
 20. A Zoo in the Basement (Christleton)
 21. The Winning Post (Christleton)

64 Saxon Sculpture Smashed and Reassembled

Position: Sandbach
Ordnance Map: Stoke-on-Trent and Macclesfield area: Sheet 118:
1/50,000
Map Ref: SJ 758/608
Access: In the centre of the Market Square: signposted from the outskirts of the town.

Sandbach's two 8th or 9th century Saxon crosses, one of the glories of Cheshire, are on a massive scale: the larger (northern) one stands over 16 feet high and the smaller 10 feet 9 inches – and these are basically only the shafts of the original crosses.

It has been deduced that the presence of the crosses points to the existence of an important Saxon church at Sandbach, one of the old minsters or monasteries through which the conversion of Saxon England was carried out. There were originally probably three crosses around the minster's site, and the two largest must have been moved into the market place either in the later Middle Ages or at the Reformation.

The first mention of them dates from 1565, when they were recorded as "two square crosses of stone on steps, with certain images and writing thereon graven". A description of the town written about 1621 fails to mention them. As a group of local Puritans had been charged with destroying a number of crosses in 1613, it is likely that they were demolished then, or possibly during the Civil War: certainly it had happened by 1660.

The fortunes which befell the fallen stones were varied: many smaller pieces were used as building material in Sandbach itself, but the two most important sculptured fragments were taken, sometime after 1670, by Sir John Crewe to his estate at Utkinton, whence they were moved to Tarporley rectory and eventually to Oulton, where they were incorporated in an artificial grotto in the park.

In 1816, as a result of the efforts of Sir John Egerton of Oulton, John Palmer and George Ormerod, the large pieces were brought back to Sandbach and reunited with other fragments recovered from various sites in the town. The two crosses were reconstructed with plain pieces of similar stone cut to shape replacing missing parts. Some additional fragments now in Sandbach churchyard are from the third, smaller, cross.

Sandbach Crosses,

65 A Famous Foxhound

Position: Sandiway
Ordnance Map: Stoke-on-Trent and Macclesfield area: Sheet 118:
1/50,000
Map Ref: SJ 608/707
Access: The Blue Cap Hotel stands on the north side of the eastbound
carriageway of the A.556 Chester-Northwich road.

Bluecap was a black-pied dog foxhound belonging to the Hon. John
Smith-Barry of Marbury Hall, whose pack was kennelled about a mile
to the east of the hotel, where the A.559 turns off from the A.556.

At this period, the 1750s, foxhounds were being bred for speed, and
Bluecap was an extremely successful product of such breeding. In his
prime, he was made to carry a weight round his neck when hunting, to
prevent him outstripping the rest of the pack.

In 1763, when Bluecap was four years old, Smith-Barry challenged the
Master of the Quorn, Hugo Meynell, to a race – any couple of Quorn
hounds against Bluecap and his daughter Wanton. The stakes were 500
guineas between the two men, with much more in side bets among the
supporters of either party.

The match, over four miles at Newmarket Heath, took place on 30th
September. The Quorn couple were favourites at 7-4, but in the end
Bluecap romped home with Wanton a close second. 100 yards behind
her came the Quorn dog, while the bitch refused to run at all.

The inn, formerly the Sandiway Head, thereupon changed its name to
commemorate Bluecap's victory for Cheshire.

The celebrated hound himself lived on for a further nine years, a local
legend in his lifetime.

Places of Interest in the Neighbourhood
50. It Floats! It Swings!! It's Electric!!! (Northwich)
66. Guardian of the Dual Carriageway (Sandiway)
76. Birthplace of the Cheshire Prophet (Whitegate)

66 Guardian of the Dual Carriageway

Position: Sandiway
Ordnance Map: Stoke-on-Trent and Macclesfield area: Sheet 117:
1/50,000
Map Ref: SJ 607/706
Access: On central reservation of dual carriageway section of A.556
road.

Whether approached from east or west the Round Tower (or Round
Lodge or Tower Lodge, as it is also known) is an unexpected sight,
seemingly a medieval watchtower marooned in the middle of a dual
carriageway. Its existence was threatened earlier this century when the
road was due to be widened from two to four lanes of traffic, but fortunately it was spared from demolition and the extra lanes were added
to the south of it.

   One local "explanation" for the reprieve is that King Charles
(whether 1st or 2nd is not revealed) hid in it while escaping (where from
is not revealed either) and that consequently it is protected by royal
charter. Picturesque, but completely untrue, as it did not even exist until
about 150 years after the Restoration.

The Round Tower, Sandiway.

Its real history is that it was built in the early 19th century as a lodge for one of the gates of the Cholmondeley family's Vale Royal estate to the south of the old road (the present eastbound carriageway). The gate itself adjoined the lodge on the west side.

Roofless now, the lodge was inhabited until about 1920. The last occupants were a family by the name of Preston. Their main living quarters were in the tower itself, and a single-storey stone extension (now demolished) on the east side served as a bedroom. Washing was performed in an outside shed. The tower used to be referred to jokingly as "the cleanest house in Sandiway" – there being no corners to harbour dirt.

Places of Interest in the Neighbourhood
51. The Old Woman of Delamere Forest (Oakmere)
65. A Famous Foxhound (Sandiway)
76. Birthplace of the Cheshire Prophet (Whitegate)

Gibbet Windmill, Great Saughall.

67 Where Irishmen Hung in Irons

Position: Saughall, north-west of Chester
Ordnance Map: Chester, Wrexham and surrounding area: Sheet 117:
1/50,000
Map Ref: SJ 363/722
Access: On the A.540, approximately 400 metres beyond the
intersection with the A.5117. There is an unsurfaced lay-by opposite
Mill Farm Shop.

The Wirral peninsula formerly contained a large number of windmills,
of which only a relatively small proportion now survive. Gibbet Mill
was described as "new-built" in 1773, and was operational for over 150
years. It functioned until 1926, and was probably the last of the Wirral
windmills to grind corn. After years of neglect, it was converted into a
private house in 1960.

A good view of the mill can be obtained by crossing a stile just to the
north and following the public footpath along the edge of the field. The
sails are copies of the originals, but reduced in size, and they do not
rotate. Apart from its architectural features, the mill is interesting for
its name, which originated as follows.

On Wednesday 29th August 1750, four itinerant Irish labourers were
walking along the main highway from Chester to Parkgate. Their
names were Garret Delany, Edward Johnson (alias Murray), John
Caffery and Bryan Molloy, an elderly man. About noon, three miles or
so from Chester, the three first-named attacked Molloy, beat him
unmercifully with their sticks, and finally cut his throat with a reaping-
hook. They took two guineas, seven shillings in silver and a bundle of
clothes done up in a handkerchief from the body, which they hid in a
ditch.

Unfortunately for the murderers, Molloy's cries had been heard by a
labourer in a nearby field, who waited for them to leave the scene, then
raised the alarm. The murderers were apprehended in the inn at Shotwick (see "Cheshire's Gretna Green"), detained overnight in a barn,
and committed to the county gaol at Chester Castle next day. Caffery
subsequently turned King's Evidence. The other two were found guilty
on 8th September and hanged at Boughton, just outside Chester, at 3
p.m. on the 22nd. That evening their bodies were "hung up in irons near
the Two Mills on the Heath, in the road to Parkgate", in the words of a
contemporary newspaper account.

Gibbet Mill must stand on or near the site of this grisly spectacle –

indeed at the time of its construction, some remains of Delany and Johnson may still have been visible.

Places of Interest in the Neighbourhood
18. One Hand on the Clock – Two Graves in the Wood (Burton)
68. Cheshire's Gretna Green (Shotwick)
77. Just the Place to Catch the Ghost Train (Willaston)

Greyhound Farm (formerly the Greyhound Inn), Shotwick.

68 Cheshire's Gretna Green

Position: Shotwick, north-west of Chester
Ordnance Map: Chester, Wrexham and surrounding area: Sheet 117:
1/50,000
Map Ref: SJ 377/718
Access: Shotwick lies west of the A.550 from North Wales to Hooton;
turn left after its junction with the A.5117. Alternatively, it can be
reached from the A.540 Chester to Neston road: turn left immediately
after the Yacht Inn, but be careful when you cross the A.550!

Shotwick today is the most secluded hamlet in Wirral, but in the 13th
century it was both a crossing-point for travellers into Wales and a port
of embarkation for Ireland.

We, however, are concerned with the latter part of the 17th century.
Greyhound Farm, on the left just before the church, was then the
Greyhound Inn, and it gained notoriety as a place where runaway
marriages were solemnised.

In 1674 one Randle Moss of Prenton appeared before the Bishop of
Chester's Court. It was said that he was "suspected to be unlawfully
married." Randle admitted that the banns had not been read either in
his parish or in that of his wife. He told the court that Mr. Heath, the
curate of Shotwick, had married them in the Greyhound Inn, a month
or five weeks before Christmas 1673.

What action the Bishop took is unrecorded, but it was apparently
ineffective, for three years later John Robinson of Bebington appeared
on a similar charge following his marriage to Isabella Mainwaring of
Eastham.

It is believed that the curate conducted a much larger number of these
irregular marriages than appear in any records, and that, furthermore,
when he was engaged elsewhere, the schoolmaster officiated in his
stead.

The Greyhound Inn (the fabric of which survives as the right-hand
part of the present house) was the place were Bryan Molloy's murderers
were apprehended (see No 67). It also appears as the "Black Bear" in a
novel by Mrs. G. Linnaeus Banks, *God's Providence House*, which is set
in Shotwick and Chester.

Places of Interest in the Neighbourhood
18. One Hand on the Clock – Two Graves in the Wood (Burton)
67. Where Irishmen Hung in Irons (Saughall)

69 Stoke Hall Dovecote

Position: Stoke, north-west of Nantwich
Ordnance Map: Stoke-on-Trent & Macclesfield area: Sheet 118:
1/50,000
Map Ref: SJ 625/569
Access: Turn east off the A.51 road on the Nantwich side of Barbridge
marina, into Stoke Hall Lane. The dovecote is in the private driveway
signed "Stoke Hall Stables", but can be viewed from the public road.

The Romans are generally credited with the introduction of dovecotes
to this country. The birds provided a welcome variation in diet, especially in winter when most livestock had been slaughtered and only
salt meat was otherwise available. As well as their flesh, the birds also
provided useful eggs, feathers and manure.

In the Middle Ages the right to possess a dovecote was confined to
lords of manors, abbots and other high ecclesiastics, though under
Elizabeth I rights of ownership were much extended, and many new
dovecotes were built in the 16th and 17th centuries.

These restrictions mean that most dovecotes today are to be found on
private estates, and this is one of the few examples locally which can be
seen from the public highway. A two-storey square brick structure, it
dates from the late 18th century. This makes it a late specimen of its
kind, for by that date the increased growing of root crops as winter feed
for cattle meant that the need for pigeon meat had declined.

The dovecote's most unusual feature is the wooden four-posted bell
turret which adorns the highest point of its slate roof.

Places of Interest in the Neighbourhood
 1. The End of the Game? (Acton)
19. The Round House (Chorley)
47. A Sacrifice Still Remembered (Nantwich)
48. From the Ashes of a Vehement Fire (Nantwich)

70 "Time Is Not All"

Position: Stretton, near Warrington
Ordnance Map: Manchester and surrounding area: Sheet 109: 1/50,000
Map Ref: SJ 620/827
Access: On the north side of the B.5356 road.

A chapel of ease at Stretton (which was then in Great Budworth parish) is stated to have been "ruinous and in decay" in 1666, but there is no information concerning its subsequent fate.

The story of the church really begins in 1826-27, when a "Commissioners' Church" was erected to designs by Philip Hardwick. This proved rather uninspiring, and in 1859 Gilbert Scott was commissioned to build a new chancel. Scott was also responsible for the rebuilding of the rest of the church in 1870-72, and so it is his design which we see today.

The most curious feature of this attractive building is its tower clock, which has two dials. Unusually for a church clock, the dials make use of letters instead of numbers. Starting at the "ten to the hour" position, that facing south reads "Forget not God", while the one facing west reads "Time is not all".

Places of Interest in the Neighbourhood
 7. Bawming the Thorn (Appleton)
25. Birthplace of Wonderland's Creator (Daresbury)
34. For Future Service or Recollection (Halton)

71 The Incomparable Penman

Position: Tarvin
Ordnance Map: Chester, Wrexham & surrounding area: Sheet 117:
1/50,000
Map Ref: SJ 492/669
Access: In centre of village.

Along the north side of St. Andrew's churchyard stands a range of
buildings, currently a parish hall and cottages. Formerly they were the
local grammar school and the schoolmaster's house. For 36 years, prior
to his death in 1740, the schoolmaster here was John Thomasen. If the
church is open, you can see his monument in the south porch.

It states that as a schoolmaster he was "approved and eminent", but
goes on to say that he was most renowned for his beautiful handwriting.

His skill with the pen brought him commissions from a number of
distinguished patrons, including Queen Anne. He was particularly
noted for his work in Greek characters, much of his output being
transcriptions from Pindar, Anacreon and Hippocrates.

In the words of his epitaph:

> "As his Incomparable performances acquired him the esteem and
> friendship of the great and learned, so his Affability and Humanity
> gained him the Good Will of all his Acquaintance, and the Decease of so
> much private worth was regretted as a public loss."

Interestingly, if his age at death (54) is correctly recorded, he became
master of Tarvin Grammar School at the age of 18.

Places of Interest in the Neighbourhood
10. The Last Great Cockfight (Ashton)
21. The Winning Post (Christleton)
36. Where Packhorses Plodded (Hockenhull Platts)

72 The Big Cheese

Position: Tattenhall
Ordnance Map: Chester, Wrexham and surrounding area: Sheet 117:
1/50,000
Map Ref: SJ 486/581
Access: Tattenhall Hall is private property, but is visible from the road,
or from the public footpath (signed) to the north-east.

Tattenhall Hall was originally built by Richard Bostock in the early
17th century, and had become a farmhouse by 1720. It was bought
in 1856 by Robert Barbour of Bolesworth Castle, who employed the
Chester architect James Harrison to restore the outbuildings and make
it into a model farm. This was done in 1860 at a cost of £1,600.

The dairy farm must have built up a considerable reputation, for in
1909 Edmund Driver, a major Bradford grocer prominent in the cheese
trade, placed an unprecedented order with Percy Cooke, the then
tenant. Mr. Driver wished to demonstrate that Cheshire cheese could be
made almost any size, and so he ordered 20 specimens, each to weigh
300 lbs. Few dairies, he said, were equal to the execution of such an
order, but Mr. Cooke and his head cheesemaker, Samuel Dickin, rose to
the occasion. Special dairy equipment had to be obtained; six large
moulds (four oak, two tin) were made to fit two large cheese presses.

For 20 consecutive days one of these monster cheeses was turned out
in the Tattenhall Hall dairy. Five of them were on view at the Chester
Cheese Fair, held on 9th June 1909. At that time the British Dairy
Farmers' Association was holding its Annual Conference in Chester,
and many members tasted the giants and testified to their excellent
quality and flavour. No Cheshire cheese approaching this weight had
been made before – the previous record is said to have been held by a
192 lb. specimen made in 1792. The experiment does not seem to have
been continued, but this was probably due more to the difficulty of
handling the monsters than any lack of skill on the part of Messrs.
Cooke and Dickin.

Places of Interest in the Neighbourhood
12. The Best of British Castramentation (Bickerton)
22. Hot Jewellery (Clutton)
55. The Elephant and Castle (Peckforton)

73 King Edward's Lost City

Position: Thelwall, between Warrington and Lymm
Ordnance Map: Manchester and surrounding area: Sheet 109: 1/50,000
Map Ref: SJ 651/875
Access: On the south side of the road junction.

On the beams beneath the eaves of the Pickering Arms can be read the words "In the year 923 King Edward the Elder founded a city here and called it Thelwall".

There is certainly not much evidence of a city in the vicinity today, and most non-locals have probably heard of Thelwall only in connection with the famous (or notorious) Viaduct.

Yet the Anglo-Saxon Chronicle records that "In this year went King Edward with a force, after harvest to Thelwall, and bade build the city and occupy and man it".

At the period in question, Edward was attempting to force the Viking leader Ragnald into submission and regain control of the northern Danelaw. What he actually ordered to be constructed at Thelwall would have been a *burh*, a fortified strongpoint of earth and timber manned by the local population, organised via the local government machinery of the shire. The object would have been to protect the important Mersey crossing at Warrington, and the date is more likely to have been 919-920 than 923.

The exact site of the *burh* is uncertain, but Thelwall's brief moment of military importance is still commemorated.

Places of Interest in the Neighbourhood
  7. Bawming the Thorn (Appleton)
44. "Careless, Intemperate and Improvident" (Lymm)
70. "Time Is Not All" (Stretton)

74 No Shelter for the Mourners Here

Position: Tilston, north-west of Malpas
Ordnance Map: Chester, Wrexham and surrounding area: Sheet 117:
1/50,000
Map Ref: SJ 457/506
Access: At the churchyard entrance on the east side of the road.

The entrance to the churchyard was the spot where the first words of
the service were read when a corpse was brought for burial. Sometimes
the whole of the service apart from the interment itself would take place
there, and so the custom grew up of constructing some shelter from the
elements for clergyman and mourners. Thus developed the lych gate
("lych" meaning corpse), usually roofed over with a canopy, and sometimes incorporating benches and/or a slab on which to rest the coffin.

Lych Gate, Tilston church.

No such refinements exist at the entrance to Tilston churchyard. Two simple ball-topped gate-piers bear the date 1687. There can be no doubt however, that this is a true lych-gate, for on the sides of both pillars is carved the symbol of the skull and crossbones.

Places of Interest in the Neighbourhood

Old Chad chapel, Tushingham.

75 Old Chad and Black Maria

Position: Tushingham, near Whitchurch
Ordnance Map: Chester, Wrexham and surrounding area: Sheet 117:
1/50,000
Map Ref: SJ 527/642
Access: By public footpath from St. Chad's Church on the A.41. The
Chapel is normally closed, but a board by the door provides
information.

Alone in a field, almost entirely forsaken now for the 'new' church built
next to the main road in 1863, stands St. Chad's chapel, known locally
as Old Chad, and originally a chapel-of-ease to the parish church at
Malpas. A chapel was recorded here in 1349, but the present building
dates from 1689-91. It is now used only for burials and occasional
services. Its isolation is partly explained by the fact that the old highway
from Chester to Whitchurch ran somewhat to the east of the present
A.41, and so would have passed close to Old Chad. Ploughing has,
however, obliterated all traces of the former road.

   In the north-west corner of the churchyard a small brick building can
be seen. This was built in 1822 as a meeting room, but a look through its
small windows shows the use to which it was put in later years. Inside
stands a fine example of a horse-drawn hearse. The Black Maria, as she
was called with a touch of grim humour, was built in 1880 by a firm at
Dodington, near Whitchurch, and was used to bring the dead for burial
at Old Chad until the 1920s.

   A visit to Old Chad, with its graves among which rabbits make their
homes, its small size and its atmosphere of peace and tranquillity, con-
jures up an old rural Cheshire far removed from the traffic rushing past
on the A.41 less than 500 metres away.

Places of Interest in the Neighbourhood
12.. The Best of British Castramentation (Bickerton)
19. The Round House (Chorley)
74. No Shelter for the Mourners Here (Tilston)

76 Birthplace of the Cheshire Prophet

Position: Whitegate, north-west of Winsford
Ordnance Map: Stoke-on-Trent & Macclesfield area: Sheet 118:
1/50,000
Map Ref: SJ 636/687
Access: Accessible by public footpath from Mill Lane to the north or
Grange Lane to the south.

Bark House is of late seventeenth century date, since restored. It is in
one of its outbuildings that Robert Nixon, the legendary Cheshire seer,
is said to have been born. Nixon's dates are uncertain, and George
Ormerod, the great Cheshire historian, went so far as to doubt his very
existence. One source states that Nixon was born at Whitsuntide 1467,
while another says that he lived in the time of James I, some 150 years
later! It was claimed that an old man who remembered him described
him as "a short squab fellow (with a) great head and goggle eyes . . . he
used to drivel as he spoke, which was very rarely, and was extremely
surly". He was reckoned little more than an idiot, and went to work as a

Bark House Farm, Whitegate.

Robert Nixon – A Conjectural Portrait.

ploughboy for Farmer Crowton of Swanlow, later being taken into the household of Thomas Cholmondeley of Vale Royal.

His "prophecies", like those of so many of his kind, were often vague and capable of a variety of interpretations. Nixon, who was renowned for his appetite, is said to have prophesied that he would die of starvation. After he had come to the attention of James I, he was summoned to the royal court, where he made a favourable impression on the "the wisest fool in Christendom", but not, apparently, on his servants. An officer had to be appointed to give him protection from their taunts and insults, and to see that he was allowed to eat his fill. Once, when the King went off hunting, Nixon's "minder" locked him up in a cupboard, allowing no one but himself to attend to the prophet's wants. When the officer received an important command from the King, he hastened to carry it out, forgetting all about Nixon. On his return three days later, the Cheshire prophet was found dead from starvation as he had predicted.

Places of Interest in the Neighbourhood
51. The Old Woman of Delamere Forest (Oakmere)
52. Imprisoned Below Stairs? (Over)
65. A Famous Foxhound (Sandiway)
66. Guardian of the Dual Carriageway (Sandiway)

Hadlow Road station, Willaston.

77 Just the Place to Catch the Ghost Train

Position: Willaston, near Neston
Ordnance Map: Chester, Wrexham and surrounding area: Sheet 117: 1/50,000
Map Ref: SJ 331/773
Access: Hadlow Road station lies on the B.5151 approximately 400 metres south of the crossroads in Willaston. "Wirral Way" signs will direct you to the car park.

The Wirral Railway's line from Hooton to Parkgate, with intermediate stations at Hadlow Road and Neston, opened on 1st October 1861. In 1866 the line was extended to West Kirby. Ninety years later it closed to passengers, and after its closure to goods in 1962 it remained unused until Cheshire County Council purchased the trackbed in 1969 to form the Wirral Way. This twelve-mile waymarked walk from West Kirby to Hooton is part of the first "country park" in Great Britain.

Pride of the line is Hadlow Road station, which has been painstakingly restored to its 1952 appearance. Track has been relaid past the platform, a signalbox erected, trolleys and luggage strategically placed, the ticket office furnished with period items of equipment, and enamel advertising signs now add colour to the station buildings.

All in all, a real treat for those who remember British Railways pre-Beeching. Only the trains are lacking!

Places of Interest in the Neighbourhood
18. One Hand on the Clock – Two Graves in the Wood (Burton)
54. Lady Hamilton and Nelson (Parkgate)
68. Cheshire's Gretna Green (Shotwick)

78 Romany's Garden of Remembrance

Position: Wilmslow
Ordnance Map: Manchester and surrounding area: Sheet 109: 1/50,000
Map Ref: SJ 846/809
Access: Off Alderley Road. Follow signs for the library: the garden is situated just to the north.

'Romany of the B.B.C.', in private life the Reverend George Bramwell Evens, was entitled to the name by which he was known as one of the most popular children's broadcasters of the 1930s and '40s. His mother was the sister of the famous evangelist Rodney 'Gypsy' Smith, and a figure second only to her brother in Methodist circles. George, who was born in Hull in 1884, himself became a Methodist minister.

A great love of nature showed itself in his personality from an early age, and the happiest years of his ministry were those spent in Carlisle, where he was able to roam the Cumbrian hills in his free time. It was in 1921, during this period, that he bought the caravan which is preserved here from gypsies at Brough Hill fair, and in it he spent his holidays thereafter.

Later, following a move to Yorkshire, he began to write nature articles for local newspapers, and it was this that led, in 1931, to a friend who worked for the B.B.C. arranging an audition for him on Children's Hour.

His broadcasts, which usually took the form on an imaginary walk with his young companions Muriel and Doris, were immensely successful, as were the books which followed. In 1939 he retired from the ministry and moved to Wilmslow to be nearer the B.B.C. studios in Manchester. On 20th November 1943 he came in from working in his garden, complained of a pain, went upstairs to rest, and died. The grief among children at the news of his death was so great that in some parts of the country schools had to close for the day.

Places of Interest in the Neighbourhood
2. The Wizard and Mr. Garner (Alderley Edge)
32. Contrasting Faces of a Baptist Chapel (Great Warford)
49. An Elizabethan Corn Mill (Nether Alderley)

Romany's caravan, Wilmslow.

79 Giants of the Chemical Industry

Position: Winnington, near Northwich
Ordnance Map: Stoke-on-Trent and Macclesfield area: Sheet 118: 1/50,000
Map Ref: SJ 642/746
Access: on the east side of Winnington Lane (A533) at the entrance to the I.C.I. Winnington Works.

Ludwig Mond and John Tomlinson Brunner first met in 1862 when they were both young men employed in the chemical works of John Hutchinson at Widnes. Their friendship deepened, and eventually they decided to set up together as soda manufacturers using the Solvay process, as opposed to the Leblanc process used by the Widnes manufacturers. Mond provided the knowledge of industrial chemistry and Brunner the financial and managerial expertise.

   After a search for a suitable site, they found and bought the Winnington Hall estate in 1872-73 and erected their first plant. Things were not easy initially. As Brunner wrote "Everything that could break down did break down, and everything that could burst did burst".

Statue of Ludwig Mond, Winnington.

Mond at this time actually lived in the works, sleeping on a bed on a platform over the engines. Both men worked six days and three nights each per week. The first soda was produced in April 1874.

From these beginnings Brunner, Mond and Co. rose to the forefront of the chemical industry, and in 1926 it merged with other large firms to form Imperial Chemical Industries.

The two founders are now commemorated life-size in bronze, in front of a rather functional-looking Research Laboratory building which it-self merits more than a passing glance. It was here, on 27th March, 1933, that R.O. Gibson, who had been conducting experiments involv-ing abnormally high pressures, made a brief entry in his laboratory notebook: "Waxy solid found in reaction tube". That waxy solid, full-scale production of which started at the nearby Wallerscote Works on the day Germany invaded Poland in 1939, was an essential element in the construction of radar sets, and after the war became a household word – polythene.

Places of Interest in the Neighbourhood

Statue of Sir John Brunner, Winnington.

80 The Time and the Inclination

Position: Wybunbury, south-east of Nantwich
Ordnance Map: Stoke-on-Trent and Macclesfield area: Sheet 118:
1/50,000
Map Ref: SJ 700/498
Access: On east side of B.5071 road.

Wybunbury tower, 96 feet high, is now a tower without a church. It was
built in the late 15th century and has seen five rebuildings of the church,
the first two of which were substantial alterations in 1595 and 1790.
Although medieval church builders were usually wise in their choice of
site, they seem to have made a serious error here, for each church has
eventually been undermined by the action of underground springs.

More than that, the springs have caused the tower to lean to the
north-east, a phenomenon first noticed about 1750. By the 1830s the
top of the tower was nearly six feet out of true, and in 1834 the body of
the church was taken down for rebuilding. The contractor was James
Trubshaw, who also built Chester's Grosvenor Bridge (at the time of
its construction the longest single-arch span in Europe). He took the
opportunity to correct the tower's lean by digging down to the old
foundations and removing sufficient clay to allow the tower to swing
back to the perpendicular.

His theory worked – for a while, anyway. But half a century later the
problems re-emerged and the church was again rebuilt in 1893. Further
evidence of structural weakness this century led to the demolition of the
chancel and the making of a new chancel out of part of the nave.

Finally, the church was pulled down in 1976 and a new, modern
church of St. Chad was built a quarter of a mile to the north. By this
date the tower was leaning again – about four feet – and becoming
unsafe.

In the late 1980s a Nottingham-based engineering firm, which had
already carried out work on the tower's better-known Pisan counter-
part, was called in. They used over 100 hydraulic jacks to take the
weight of the tower while a new foundation was constructed and the
structure stabilised, the work being completed in 1989.

Although there is built-in provision to correct any future leaning
tendencies, it was decided to leave the tower with a "designer slant" of
eighteen inches to two feet to enable it to retain its locally unique
character.

St Chad's tower, Wybunbury.

Places of Interest in the Neighbourhood
11. Butchers, Butter and Bears (Audlem)
47. A Sacrifice Still Remembered (Nantwich)
48. From the Ashes of a Vehement Fire (Nantwich)

Index

Places by Page number